In every age, the church is called to enfle and place. But for Christians to do so effectively, they will need to understand their unique time and place and, especially, the neighbors who inhabit it with them. The Row House Forum is just such a "roadmap" for thoughtful Christians, as well as a gathering place for all who are intellectually hungry. Every Christian community would benefit from such a forum.
—Katelyn Beaty, *Christianity Today* editor-at-large, book author,
    2016 forum speaker for The Row House

The Row House proves that it is possible to engage in conversations about culture with authenticity, curiosity, and uncommon graciousness. In *Good Posture* Tom invites us behind these conversations to hear his heart for building better bridges and practicing insane kindness. Rooted in the Gospel, this book will help you engage in thoughtful conversations and create a more attractive way of impacting culture.
—Peter Greer, president & CEO HOPE International
    and 2014 forum speaker for The Row House

Tom Becker is a man living a life that leaves a mark. Through a heavenly blend of humor, grace, whimsy, and gospel, Tom offers readers the opportunity to reassess their approach to the world around them. Shall we approach life hunched over and believing the worst about our neighbors, or standing tall, looking for the best in those around us? I know which approach sounds more life-giving and Kingdom bearing to me. Read this book, and follow Tom's work to readjust your perspective, and your posture."
—Luke Dooley, former Director of Q Commons at Qideas

In *Good Posture,* Tom Becker encourages us to lean into life so we can flourish where we are, for God's glory and the common good. He tells the story of The Row House in Lancaster, PA not so we all start one but as a living example of bringing grace into the heart of a city. In the process Becker distills what he has learned, and the distillation is a lovely dose of biblical wisdom. It's a vision of the sort of Christianity we always hoped was possible but rarely see. It's a vision not of beginning something big but of being faithful and watching the gospel nurture beauty in ordinary people in ordinary ways.
—Denis Haack, co-founder of Ransom Fellowship
    and the editor of *Critique* magazine

Tom is the kind of conversationalist who cares more about listening than being heard. But you also come away from talking with him somehow more full of ideas and hopes and dreams. His listening is the kind that inspires.
—Wesley Hill, author of *Paul and the Trinity: Persons, Relations, and the Pauline Letters* and 2015 forum speaker for The Row House

The Row House Forum serves the public good in one of the best ways possible: by promoting ideas, art, conversation, and human flourishing. It's a gift to the local community, as well as a gift from the local community to the world. The Row House Forum is a jewel whose brilliance reaches far and wide.
—Karen Swallow Prior, PhD, author of *Booked: Literature in the Soul of Me* and 2017 forum speaker for The Row House

Tom's hospitality, insight, and sense of fun came to life in the pages of *Good Posture.* As someone lucky enough to attend many Row House events, I can say with delight that this book will give you a taste of what it's like to be welcomed into a community by Tom, and some starting points for living out that generous hospitality in your own context.
—Hannah Eagleson, writer/editor for InterVarsity's Emerging Scholars Network and 2013 forum speaker for The Row House

I have known Tom Becker for many years and have been simply stunned at his energy and insight, verve and fidelity in doing what he is called to do—which he describes with wit and wonder in this easy-to-read, one-of-a-kind book. *Good Posture* is influenced by everything from the Bible and the Beatles to Francis Schaeffer and modern art films. May this book inspire you to loosen up a bit, check your posture, and then take up the wild, wondrous adventure of gracious Christian living in our lovely, messy world.
—Byron Borger, co-founder of Hearts & Minds Bookstore

C.S. Lewis aptly said that if we read history carefully, we will soon discover that those who have done the most good for the present world are the ones who thought the most of the next. My long-time friend, Tom Becker, does a marvelous job calling us back to this vision in *Good Posture.* I couldn't recommend this book more highly. Please read it cover to cover. Please share it. And please, for the love of God, start living it.
—Scott Sauls, senior pastor of Christ Presbyterian Church (Nashville) and author of *Jesus Outside the Lines, Befriend,* and *From Weakness to Strength*

GOOD POSTURE

GOOD POSTURE

ENGAGING CURRENT CULTURE
WITH ANCIENT FAITH

TOM BECKER

In Christian art, the square halo
identified a living person
presumed to be a saint.
Square Halo Books is devoted
to publishing works that present
contextually sensitive biblical studies
and practical instruction consistent
with the Doctrines of the Reformation.
The goal of Square Halo Books is to
provide materials useful for encouraging
and equipping the saints.

Photo of Tom by Chelsea Batten
Painting of The Row House by William Becker

First Edition 2017
Copyright ©2017 Square Halo Books
P.O. Box 18954, Baltimore, MD 21206
www.SquareHaloBooks.com

ISBN 978-1-941106-08-2
Library of Congress Control Number: 2017960987

Printed in the United States of America.

To the
love of my
earthly life,
**REBECCA
JOHNSON
BECKER**,
May 18, 1985:
Happy Perpetual
Anniversary!

CONTENTS

WHAT I DO

TO REMEMBER THE PAST IS TO SEE THAT WE ARE HERE
TODAY BY GRACE, THAT WE HAVE SURVIVED AS A GIFT.

—Frederick Buechner, *A Room Called Remember: Uncollected Pieces*

I won't forget the humid July afternoon I first saw our three-story row home on College Avenue in Lancaster, Pennsylvania. Stepping up onto the generous wooden porch, I glanced left and right and noticed a stretch of similar porches opening up to my sight, all the way up the block. A true, walkable neighborhood. A place to know and be known. A future home.

Stepping into the house over the marble threshold, I looked up to see a glass transom encased in Pennsylvania hardwoods and painted dozens of times. I stepped into a tiny foyer and through a second interior door with lace curtains. What I felt was a handshake. And I don't mean with my realtor Jack Hess. That would come later. Rather, vertical dwellings such as a modest row house, built to a human scale, have a way of saying, "Hi! I'm kinda like you. Welcome!" I didn't hear an audible voice that day, but I will say I was eager to show 413 College Avenue to my wife Becky and our oldest three kids (ages twelve, ten, and eight).

Jack, my former college housemate, was a native Lancastrian. He was willing to show me any of the myriad properties in Lancaster County, but we had narrowed the search down: close to Franklin & Marshall College with shops and stops close by. I was being asked to restart Reformed University Fellowship in the Lancaster area, either at F&M or Millersville University—whichever came first. Being near a college was a requirement. Our second search criterion was more like a strong preference: walkability. Suffice to say that in our former lives, we enjoyed the density of Lewisburg, another fine college town in Pennsylvania. After assessing the house, I strolled across the street. Passing the North Museum of Natural History and the F&M Arts building, I found myself on a crest overlooking a wonderful, tree-filled park named for James Buchanan. I saw a gleaming new playground. I considered our youngest ones, William and Maggie (ages three and a half and one), sat down to cool off, and wept for joy.

The aluminum screen door out front would have to go, the sagging third-floor ceiling would need to be replaced immediately, and the pink shag carpet blanketing the living room required a new home in a dump. But overall, the solid brick Victorian would make a great home. I had no idea that one day, eleven years later, my wife Becky would suggest we name my life's work after that little row house. The name "The Row House" fit immediately, again, like a firm and warm handshake. But what *is* The Row House? Before I get to that, I must explain a bit of my pre-Lancastrian history.

For my entire adult life, I've devised clever strategies on trains or at conferences to avoid the question: "So, what do you do for a living?" My main tactic is to get to the question first by asking a diversionary one of my own meant to steer the conversation away from my career for just enough time to pull away for more coffee or say "Look at the time. Gotta go!" Most of my friends and family members can give an answer that allows someone to size them up by having at least a notion of their job: my parents were Store Owners. My brothers are a Diesel Mechanic and Plant Safety Manager, respectively. I have friends who are Counselors, Pastors, Project Managers, Graphic Designers, and Musicians.

My job title from 1985–1995 was Campus Minister. Most people, especially outside the evangelical church culture, have no mental map for grasping what I've done. I would include my parents in that category. At the antique auctions, it was tough for them to tell their comrades just what I did. "Tom's down there at Bucknell. He does church things with the kids." To their credit they have unswervingly supported me. But I simply couldn't get Mom to recite: *"Tom's an InterVarsity staff worker, specializing in training student leaders to build and lead Christian fellowships on their campuses."* Thankfully, I was ordained in the Presbyterian Church in America in 2000, and she could say with certainty, "Our Tom's a Pastor down in Lancaster." It all got squirrely, though, when folks asked where my church was. Because, to make life difficult, of course, I didn't have a church. My "field" was the campus of Millersville University.

By this time, however, I was comfortable saying (and explaining) that I was a Campus Pastor. After R.U.F., I taught in a classical Christian school for four years. Finally, something conventional. "I'm a teacher," or, depending on the audience, I could say, "I'm a realtor," because I did, in fact, earn my sales license and worked for a brokerage for two years. All of that predictability went out the window the day I founded The Row House, Inc. Now I would no longer be able to say that I'm a Pastor, Teacher, or Realtor. I'd have to say, "Uh, I started an organization that . . . ." Sputtering, floundering, and backtracking my way to the coffee.

After six years, I do have my elevator speech pretty clearly rehearsed. I tell people I run an organization in Lancaster City that engages current cultural topics with the Christian faith. If I'm in a place hip enough to handle it, I say, "I'm a Curator." I've realized over the years that since I was a lad, I've been curating events and experiences for others. What started as a very lame "Beatles Fest" in my garage at the age of sixteen that drew exactly five people, led to providing dance music at high schools, hosting college skit nights, and generally being the guy that gets on the mic in front of a crowd for any reason. I also enjoy leading worship in our church, a task requiring a fair amount of learned modesty and seriousness.

Nowadays, I enjoy talking about what I *do,* even if I can't always explain who I *am* to the satisfaction of my questioners. It helps that our forums draw anywhere from twenty-five to two hundred people, and we see new people each night. With online resources, who knows how many more people we are reaching, "engaging current culture with ancient faith." Curating, it turns out, is my life's work.

A meandering stream led me to this point of vocational fit. Along the way the stream turned into Bunyan's Slough of Despond: Becky had suffered exhaustion-induced anxiety and depression; the campus ministry job unceremoniously ended due to a funding shortfall; my faculty contract at the classical Christian school was not renewed; and pastoral jobs I had hoped to secure (even one in my own local congregation) did not materialize. I was completely out of ideas of what I could do to support my family. I had soldiered through it all, but wasn't aware how emotionally burned out I had become. We had five kids, one in college, and one about to get married, and I was in no condition to search for jobs again. Perhaps I'd have to dig deep and discover who I really was at age forty-seven.

I knew God would provide for us through me, but I had no imagination for it as I sat among the smoldering embers of my life. I found that I would often cry at the drop of a hat. According to my dear doctor friend, Dr. Steve Wilbraham, I was suffering from PTSD. He prescribed Lexapro for me to take the edge off my racing, anxious brain.

I began riding my bicycle eight miles to school (I had to finish out the school year with what felt like a millstone hanging around my neck). On one particular ride through the Amish farmlands I suddenly noticed that my mind had jumped out of the rut of negative preoccupation. Amazingly, I found myself thinking of something besides my family's destitution. The medication had begun to ease my adrenal system, apparently. Two other provisions injected energy back into me, as well. First, my parents paid off the remainder of our mortgage. We had no savings or severance, so this gift gave us a path forward for staying in Lancaster, our hearts' desire. Then, I found out through a savvy administrator at the school that I was eligible for unemployment compensation. I had never even considered that option. But it worked. With eighteen months of unemployment compensation, I tried to find other positions, and I also drew up a vision for a work I could take with me anywhere. It would give me something to work on. Just thinking about The Row House renewed my hope that I could be useful to others, and this helped bring me back from the brink of despair.

By the time our eldest daughter Katie was married I could say that I was finally back to my rascally, idea-driven/task-oriented self. But there would be relapses into fear, self-loathing, and depression into the following year. My only recourse during that season was to actually *do* something. I improved the Row House vision statement. I envisioned a hospitality-driven outreach centered on outstanding Christian lectures, food, and fun. I knew I could do that, even in my weakness. Whether or not people would attend or support it was not part of the question because I needed to "be me and do good" in my context.[1] I did have experience hosting similar events over the years. Back at Bucknell, I curated a campuswide lecture series through our Christian fellowship, called "Hope for the Nineties." It seems I was very forward-thinking, even in 1988. Topics ranged from mental health to intelligent design and featured local and statewide academicians, one a prominent meteorology researcher from Penn State. Attendance varied, and though I wasn't thrilled with the results, it sure beat the Beatle Fest of '78.

After all my years on college campus, and the four years in a terrific Christian school environment, I knew that deep down, I needed to create something unique. While still in recovery from my anxiety, I began hosting talks in our home. My speakers were friends whom I trusted as sound Christian thinkers or noteworthy Christian practitioners. We would sometimes jam thirty-five people into our dining room and library, a few standing in the foyer, a couple awkwardly positioned on the steps! I was the first Row House speaker. My topic was exceedingly personal: *Stability in an Age of Mobility.* I drew on Benedictine ideals and made reference to Jonathan Wilson-Hartgrove's book on the importance of Christians rooting themselves as a means to holiness.[2] This was my story: come hell or high water, we would stay in Lancaster to root, shoot, and bear fruit, unless we were clearly called elsewhere.

The Row House was not really a novel project. Several years earlier Ned Bustard had joined me in launching *The Ivory Tower: A Common Sense Forum on Arts and Culture* at a local Borders Books & Music. I drew on those instincts and my memories from the three months our family spent in England at a residential study center called L'Abri. It was a great success at building a bridge between Christians and seekers in a public setting. We produced provocative posters with snappy titles like "What the Elephant Man Taught Me About Human Dignity," "The Death of Great Sex," "Bad Art: The Problem of Evil in the Creative Process," "Draco Malfoy is My Hero," "The Beauty of Baseball," "Getting to the Heart of Race Relations in Lancaster," "After Eden: Thoughts About Life, Death, and God while Weeding," and "Biological Warfare in the Post-Human World," to name a few. We had fun with it. But in hindsight, one thing was clear from *The Ivory Tower:* college campus ministry was never going to be wide and wild enough for me. I longed to do more in and around my neighborhood with a diverse audience. My creative curator instincts were itching to emerge; I just didn't know it. I had to emerge from the slough of despond to see the celestial city on the horizon.

Which gets back to "What is The Row House, Inc., anyway?" Here's the elevator pitch:

OUR VISION
To engage current culture
with ancient faith

OUR MISSION
To host public gatherings
in Lancaster City that
present a Christian viewpoint
on critical cultural ideas,
movements, and people.

OUR APPROACH
We encourage civil discussion,
value live experiences,
showcase local presenters, and
create memorable settings.

I've written this book to describe what I've seen and heard in the process of launching, directing, and improving The Row House, Inc. I've organized this book into parts around the four-strand DNA found in our approach: *civility, hospitality, personality,* and *creativity.* The chapters within each of the four parts lay out some concepts to assist you in cultural engagement. As illustrations of those concepts I'll tell some stories from Lancaster.

This book is not a handbook for missions, evangelism, or apologetics. All of these are critical tasks for the church and individuals to study and undertake. Rather, I want you to consider what Christian cultural engagement should look like, feel like, even smell like. What should our posture as Christ followers be in this historical moment? To what extent are we affected by our culture or affecting it? How can we improve our cultural approach? I'm not writing a manifesto or a battle cry to Christian warfare. I'm calling us to embrace our humanity in all its ruinous, glorious potential through Christ. As Ken Myers of Mars Hill Audio puts it, "culture is what we make of the world." If The Row House is anything, it is my theater for showing what good, beautiful, and truthful culture-making can look like. It's a big boast for a small-town boy like me, but here I stand.

I've chosen to leave the classical discussion of apologetic nuance to more capable minds than my own. So many other books have been written on this, many you should take note of in the Discussion Questions at the end of the book. My passion is not for Christians to use culture to proclaim a Christian message. That is mere instrumentality. Rather, I want to inspire the creating, sustaining, and envisioning of generative culture reform.[3] I realize that no matter how winsome our overall presentation of Christian faith is, misunderstanding and bad faith will still be directed toward us. That's nothing new; in fact, it's one of Jesus' assumptions for His disciples. At the same time, by adorning the verbal proclamation of the Good News of Jesus with civility, hospitality, personality, and creativity, we are making His call "attractive," as Paul says.[4]

The stakes are high. The twenty-first century has proven already that earthlings don't always get along well. We must embrace civility. We are increasingly joining tribes and erecting walls. We must not forget hospitality. We are living more and more as digitally-saturated souls in physical exile. We must recover our personhood. We can barely discern the the faint glimmer of joy we once tried to capture in a jar when we were children. We must allow the creative spark to once again hold us spellbound.

ENDNOTES

1. A book that came to affirm and vindicate much of what I had done in building The Row House, Inc. is Jonathan Golden's *Be You Do Good* (Grand Rapids, MI: Baker Books, 2016). I can't recommend this book too highly for anyone needing to be freed from mere provision, obligation, or expectations in their work to do what God has fitted them to do.

2. Jonathan Wilson-Hartgrove, *The Wisdom of Stability: Rooting Faith in a Mobile Culture* (Brewster, MA: Paraclete Press, 2010).

3. Makoto Fujimura, *Culture Care: Reconnecting with Beauty for Our Common Life* (Downers Grove, IL: InterVarsity Press 2011).

4. Titus 2:10, (New International Version).

CIVILITY

QUICK TO LISTEN

AND THEY SAT WITH HIM ON THE GROUND SEVEN DAYS
AND SEVEN NIGHTS, AND NO ONE SPOKE A WORD TO HIM,
FOR THEY SAW THAT HIS SUFFERING WAS VERY GREAT.

—Job 2:13 ESV

In 2016 I helped a close friend campaign for a political office. "My opponent has been in office for twenty-five years, and has run unopposed for the past six elections." Rob's words startled me. He's a supremely likable fellow who, in turn, likes everyone else. So it was tough for me to imagine him having an opponent. But in politics, as in sports, you must face your opponents. Rob knocked on ten thousand doors in Lancaster City and spent countless hours listening to residents. I joined him on a few of those humid summer afternoons. I observed him speaking with grace and humor in debates, avoiding potshots at his opponent and, more importantly, distancing himself from his own presidential candidate who was was not exactly kind or predictable. Rob waged a war of civility and garnered a third of the votes he needed to win.

According to Dan Spanjer and Amy Black, two lecturers we hosted in Lancaster before that election cycle, the political middle in both major parties has been shrinking. "No Compromise" has supplanted "Compromise" as the most effective rallying cry in getting votes. When's the last time any of us witnessed political opponents listening carefully to each other in order to clarify issues and find common ground? Christians of all kinds get tossed back and forth within their own parties between the poles. 2016 got pretty tribal.

Sebastian Junger suggests we are hardwired for tribalism.[1] Tribes are what give us purpose, identity, and community. His main illustrations are drawn

from recent military campaigns. Soldiers returning from the tight-knit broth-
erly action of the Afghan front find themselves home: in shallow communities, bereft of the purpose they once had. The enemy without no longer exists.
They miss their band of brothers. Then, the enemy within raises its head and
launches an ambush. Depression, self-medication of all kinds, and loneliness
turn up their assault. Until and unless a returned soldier finds a replacement
tribe, his reintegration into civilian life will be laced with land mines. Liberal
societies like ours have given tribalism a bad rap, but Junger is saying we have
an evolutionary determination to seek tribe. We're losing our core identity to
our own self-destructive lust for personal space and independence. I find his
argument compelling, if self-contradictory. If we're wired for tribe, and we are
evolving biologically and societally, why are so many of us lonesome? Isn't it
more likely that our wires are so crossed that we easily drift away from community unless we're compelled by a common enemy? And couldn't tribalism
itself lead to xenophobia, warfare, and genocide? History holds the answer. Still,
his application to our desperation to belong is something ancient faiths have
addressed for millennia.

Tribe (spiritually speaking) is nothing new to Jesus and His followers.
Christianity is founded upon unity, both globally and locally. Christians have
also fallen prey to lesser tribes such as nationalism, racism, classism, and sex-
ism. Still, the tribe toolbox is in their truck. If only believers would use their
tools to build bridges instead of walls. When we build a bridge, something
beautiful happens: the lost and wounded can find a place to belong. There
is a battle in the Christian faith, but the lines aren't the same as the political
ones. Jesus drew His own lines with a sword and still does, but we must ask
ourselves: whose side are we on? Aren't we called to peace? Who really are
our enemies?

I'm reminded of one of those mysterious portions of Scripture in the story
of Jericho. It's similar to the scene J.R.R. Tolkien paints in *The Fellowship of the
Ring*. Tom Bombadil lands in that story as if from heaven, and departs just
as abruptly with no explanation. In Scripture, Joshua was out looking over
the battle lines for the next day's conquest against the walled city. Suddenly,
"a man was standing before him with drawn sword in his hand." Being the
commander of Israel, Joshua rightly asked whose side the man was on. He
replies, "No; but I am the commander of the army of Yahweh. Now I have
come."[2] Joshua must've been thinking, "Wait. I'm the commander, right?" The
Bombadil character, who we can surmise was an angelic being, answered

Joshua's question on his own terms. "Forget whose side I'm on. I'm a messenger of the Lord." Joshua hit the ground in worship, and the angel informed Joshua he was standing on holy ground. Joshua slipped off his sandals.

One of our main tag lines for The Row House is "Nothing is Not Sacred." I don't mean by this that we live in a wholly holy world. Rather, I'm affirming that we live in a sin-saturated world where God chooses to show up, and no corner of this sphere is off-limits to Him. When He appears, He leaves footprints of holiness. In a spiritual sense, our world is Chernobyl being taken back by nature. Christ is redeeming all things at this very moment, and His intentions are holiness for every square inch of creation. This reclamation project is centered on humanity. The raw material He's working with are "jars of clay," much like Joshua. His real opponents are the sentient beings, both human and angelic, who oppose Him. But that's His business. Whose side are we on as we set out to engage culture? Where is the holy God in all this? And who are our enemies? If we can answer these questions, we will be proper servants of God in battles raging around us.

If our Lord has enemies, we are bound to as well. But so what? How does He treat them? With embarrassing mercy. Our business then, following in the steps of the Son of Man, is to love our enemies, to pray for our persecutors, and to extend mercy to all in His name. That mercy includes civility toward those who aren't yet on board with His cleanup project. We don't have a right to ignore people. As James the brother of Jesus put it, "Be quick to listen and slow to speak." The nursery expression holds true: God gave us two ears but one mouth. Anyone made in God's image is worthy of respect and a listening ear. How else can we bring a message suitable to their longings and questions?

At The Row House, our first line in the defense of listening is with our speakers. I only invite thinkers and practitioners whom I feel are good listeners. Perhaps they've studied long and hard on their topic. Perhaps they possess a self-moderated posture of listening to others in conversation. Perhaps they are more eager to learn from others than to hear themselves talk. A return speaker who demonstrates listening well is Phillip Johnston. Wise beyond his age, Phillip reads widely with a passion for lived wisdom. No wonder, then, that his forums are not only memorable but also eclectic. Topics have ranged from Terence Malick's *Tree of Life* to "How Extroverts Can Help Introverts." He's one of the introverts, by the way. I've found some of the sharpest Christian communicators are. Mr. Johnson now works out his love for ideas and people at a Christian residential study center founded by Francis and Edith Schaeffer called L'Abri—French for "shelter." There, in Jane Austen's backyard in rural England, Phillip hosts a stream of meal discussions and leads a host of mentoring relationships, all rooted in the discipline of listening well to others' questions about anything under the sun.

Besides inviting presenters who listen well as a matter of course, my second concern is for listening to rule our live events. Speaking of Francis A. Schaeffer, the story goes that he was asked, "Given an hour on a train with a stranger, how would you spend it?" He remarked that he'd probably ask questions for fifty minutes. Then, as time and appropriateness dictated, he would proclaim the Good News of Jesus to points of tension or interest in the other person.[3] In The Row House Forums, I have tried to demonstrate civility in one simple way: I lay down ground rules before the presenter speaks. First, we ask that she receive our utmost attention for the duration of the talk. Then, as we open up the floor for brief questions, I request the audience members to refrain from commentary. I also ask that each participant listen to the other members with the same degree of attention they wish others would give them. I'm not merely trying to defuse craziness in our forums, though that is, honestly, a goal too. I'm desiring to demonstrate civility. More than that, I want to encourage "speaking the truth in love," as the Apostle Paul frames our obligation as Christian communicators.

Interestingly, Paul's injunction to civil conduct was written to *Christians in Ephesus,* and wasn't directed at how they should speak in public. He wants them to simply get along with each other, from the heart. Getting Christians to act kindly often is half the battle. In the broader world, Christians tend to have a reputation for speaking before listening. Since our forums are meant for the public, I'm less concerned with a guest, newcomer, or committed skeptic speaking up—it's the Christians that make me nervous. There are not too many Christ-centered events where anyone can ask a question and not feel ashamed or fear being run out on a rail. I thought my forums, with their punchy titles and inviting marketing, would spark more fireworks. Most, though, are quite civil. Disagreeable folks, I suppose, are shamed into keeping my ground rules. Perhaps, it's also true that those with honest and hard questions just aren't ready to share what's on their mind from fear of past smackdown. You know what I'd love to overhear in a coffee shop someday? "Go to the Row House. They have the biggest ears around."

I studied Rhetoric as an undergraduate. That is an uppity way of saying I majored, along with six others, in Speech/Communications. I have since taught a course on interpersonal Communication for groups, inspired in part by my enjoyable courses at Bloomsburg University of Pennsylvania. My favorite form of torture, therefore, is the Role Play. They are exceedingly awkward in college, and no less unnerving in any other setting. Still, they're effective at making us aware of communication realities. In one such role play, I was paired with a blonde, buxom sorority girl whose name I somehow can't remember. Let's call her Buffy. To say I did not traverse her orbit while at university would be an understatement. We were asked to interview each other about our upbringing, sitting back to back. Obviously, we were paying attention to nonverbal communication, or the lack thereof. The second role play with Buffy involved conducting a "natural" conversation in which we were to restate each other's comments before asking our own questions about them. For instance, "So, you were raised in the Poconos, and your Mom was your third grade teacher. Did I get that right?" If your partner felt adequately listened to in that exchange, they would then permit you to say something about yourself. Awkward and difficult.

A few years later, the Conversational Skills Rating Scale (CSRS) was developed and it became the benchmark for gauging the quality of interpersonal communication.[4] The areas measured are Attentiveness, Composure, Expressiveness, and Coordination. It's as if nothing is new under the sun. Be quick to listen; slow to speak. Speak the truth in love. In keeping with that measuring stick, how good are we at paying attention, maintaining self-control, expressing ourselves in appropriate ways, and coordinating the various elements of our communicative events with grace?

Are Christians known for their listening skills? I believe in some circles, yes, but it's not our calling card. We may have the toolbox, but the trick is putting the tools to use. Without love for our fellow earthlings, we don't even open the box. One of the reasons I started hosting forums was to venture out on this bridge of commonsense communication, park the truck, and start some repairing.

ENDNOTES

1. Sebastian Junger, *Tribe: On Homecoming and Belonging,* (New York: Hachette Book Group, 2016.

2. Joshua 5:13ff (English Standard Version).

3. Will Metzger, *Tell the Truth: The Whole Gospel Wholly by Grace Communicated Truthfully and Lovingly* (Downers Grove, IL: InterVarsity Press 2012).

4. The CSRS was developed by Brian Spitzberg, a professor of communication at San Diego State University.

SLOW TO SPEAK

ANGRY WORDS WON'T STOP THE FIGHT
TWO WRONGS WON'T MAKE IT RIGHT.
A NEW HEART IS WHAT I NEED.
OH, GOD MAKE IT BLEED.

—Paul David Hewson, "Like a Song,"
from the album *War* by U2

Departing south from Zurich by train, a jaw-dropping view opens up to the traveler: a concrete bridge spanning a granite gorge, peppered with clumps of clinging pine trees. The train takes a curve and crosses the span through wisps of clouds, effortlessly.

The bridge seems unimpressed by the razor-sharp stones around it, by the childish moods of the river and the contorted, ugly grimaces of the rock face. It stands content to reconcile the two sides of the ravine like an impartial judge, modest and willingly literal-minded about its own achievements, ashamed lest it detain our attention or attract our gratitude.[1]

I'm indebted to one of my mentors, Jerram Barrs, for instilling in me the image of bridge-building. Building bridges instead of walls applies to civility in general and Christian proclamation in particular. We are easily reminded, if we'll see it, that even the most bold communicators of spiritual truths build bridges to their hearers. Prophets enacted performances. Jesus spoke in parables. Paul improvised from Greek poets and philosophers. Throughout church history, luminaries found ways to embrace the God-instilled memories of glory in their culture to present Christ. Patrick loved the earth and its fruits and con-veyed the Savior's teachings in elegant ways, germane to his adopted Ireland. To build bridges in our culture is to resist the drift toward propaganda, a prac-tice which only exploits the basest of human desires. The basest one is pride. Pride gives rise to obsessive control. *Triumph of the Will* was produced by the Third Reich to excite nationalism and Arian supremacy. In a way, Hitler built elegant bridges.[2] He was obsessed with design and architecture as a means to power, but his goal was not the Kingdom of God. Propaganda seeks to control the traffic on the bridge. But Christian communicators seek no such control. We build a bridge between what we are hearing from God and the God-made people we are trying to reach. Hopefully it's an elegant bridge, strong and mod-est and beautiful. But we can't control the traffic. We can't make people think, feel, or act a certain way. "We refuse to practice cunning," as the crafty Paul puts it (2 Corinthians 4:2). Our purpose as Christian communicators is not to control communication or its outcomes, but to find the most effective, human-honoring ways to proclaim Christ.

Not only must we avoid falling prey to propaganda ourselves, we must beware its relative weaknesses, lest we get too freaked out by its bombast. In 1988, *The Last Temptation of Christ* was released in select theaters. Film stu-dents and open-minded viewers were somewhat interested in this retelling of the life of Jesus. It portrayed Christ as just another human: doubting His iden-tity, crushingly in love with Mary Magdalene, and foundering in His lead-up to the cross. The Christian airwaves were tingling with the news of this hereti-cal portrayal of the perfect Savior of the world. I was not living in Lancaster County at the time, as I was busy in rural Pennsylvania working with students at Bucknell University. Through my colleagues, however, I heard about one Lancaster church's boycott of a showing of the film at Franklin & Marshall College. Their approach seemed off-kilter to me, and it wasn't until I thought more about various approaches to culture that I understood why.

Richard Neibuhr, in his oft-quoted *Christ and Culture*,[3] classified the three basic ways Christians have approached culture through the lens of faith in Christ. I'll be using my own labels in some cases:

OPPOSITION (Christ fighting culture)

AGREEMENT (Christ accepting culture)

SYNTHESIS (Christ engaging culture)

Within the synthesis approach, in which Christ is involved yet distinct from human culture, there are three sub-approaches. As you read these, consider if you have have seen them in action:

SUPERNATURAL (Christ without culture)

DUALISTIC (Christ paralleling culture)

TRANSFORMATIONAL (Christ changing culture)

The *supernaturalist* Christ is involved with culture from above. He is unaffected, existing in His own impermeable realm. Thomas Aquinas is associated with this view. The *dualist* Christ exists in constant tension with culture, vying with human authorities. Luther's law and gospel approach to reality is suited to this view. And, finally, the *transformational* Christ is the view we see in Augustine and Calvin: He is embedded in His world with His church, restoring all things in a mysterious yet observable way.

Niebuhr offers these postures as legitimate Christian responses, depending on the setting. Looking at groups of believers in Scripture, for instance, you can see that some circumstances call for advance, some for retreat, and some for entrenchment. The language of warfare is fitting even if it makes some of us queasy. The point is, Christians are continuously juggling the call to seek peace, to take a stand, or to burrow ourselves down into our world.

We can see several of these approaches in the film boycott at the college. Being familiar with the congregation in question, it was clear to me that the church picketers believed in the Christ of transformation. Certainly some in their ranks had honest and caring intentions to uphold the historic, apostolic teachings that undergird Christian orthodoxy. The reality, however, is that they crouched into a stance of Christ *fighting* culture. No matter how you boycott something or demonstrate your opposition using signs, you are creating an "us versus them" ethos. That was the sock in the gut I was feeling when I heard about their boycott. Admittedly, as one who loves the Jesus of the New Testament record and who has had his deepest affections transformed by His personal touch, I too was wary of the film. The church demonstration provoked me and has stuck with me as a lesson of what it might mean for Christians to demonstrate listening and speaking in our world.

First, the church folk constructed a flimsy bridge. To arrive from the surrounding county to voice a complaint on a campus is kind of like an Amish group picketing a hospital. It's possible a few of the demonstrators either lived near or worked on the campus. Perhaps one or two attended the college years ago. But for the most part, the band was other. I wake up each morning and look out over this same campus. I have since 1999. If picketers of any kind were to show up, I would question their motives. What makes you feel you can speak into this situation? Are you invested in this community? Are you just here to embolden your own sense of commitment to a cause?

Compare a picketing line to Michael Murray. He came to F&M in the mid 1980s as a high-energy, youthful philosophy professor. I met him at a fraternity on Bucknell's campus. He had been invited to speak to the brothers about the epistemological contributions of Christian faith or some such apologetic discourse. I remember vividly that Mike was a respected scholar/teacher who laid his life down for undergraduates on a daily basis. I wonder, on the day of the picket, how he felt if he peered down from his office in Stager Hall at the bobbing placards on the sidewalk. I picture him returning to his office seat and swiveling back to his desk, head buried in his hands.

Second, they built a bridge to nowhere. It was only a movie. Art is a powerful reflection of the human condition and the individuals who create it. But most honest media watchers now admit that art rarely transforms people. Instead, it *expresses* more than it impresses. Since the rise of Pietism in the late nineteenth century, zealous Christians have made too much of these mediums, not allowing them to be the expression point of doubt, unbelief, and longing. Though films can move our emotional needles to seismic proportions, they do very little to change our assumptions, convictions, or choices. Even *Triumph of the Will* couldn't save Nazism from internal unrest. A film that shows a human, albeit sinfully human, side of Christ is no more destructive to His character than the comedy *Life of Brian*. Neither of these popular art pieces moved the needle of Christendom a hair. They did, however, express a questioning of church authority and dogma. They kept Jesus in our popular culture and, in the Monty Python film, offered a humorous insight into crowd psychology. Similarly, *The Passion of the Christ* by Mel Gibson in 2004 engendered in many Christians an expectation of global revival. Though critically acclaimed, generously endowed, and meticulously executed, *The Passion* turned out to be a great film that showcased Gibson's zeal for Roman Catholicism. But no revival came.

Third, the demonstrations drew attention away from the many elegant bridges already in service. The real opportunity for cultural transformation goes on in the classrooms. For many years, professors have gotten away with dismissing revealed religion such as Christianity as lacking any relevance to modern problems. Enlightenment reigns, and supernaturalists are ridiculed as a matter of course. It is into that arena that many Christians, thankfully, have immersed themselves in order to dial back the *anthro-theism* of the modern university. In steps Michael Murray, not just metaphorically. Convinced Christians are once again part of the campus culture, not as evangelists, but as cultural ambassadors. And the Beckers are still here on College Avenue. I haven't seen any protests lately by outsiders. But if I ever do, I'll keep my distance, and say a prayer for the Christians who are embedded there on the bridge.

These days we can select the kind of religious content we hear. And most people can avoid the challenge to consider God. In the busy downtown of Pittsburgh, a stone pulpit lurches out over the sidewalk on Sixth Avenue. Built as part of the exterior of the imposing structure in 1903, presiding ministers would occasionally address gathering throngs where now cars bustle by. Gathering a crowd these days to hear a biblical exhortation usually requires a Jerk. This fellow, usually male, Fundamentalist, and angry, continues to ply his trade on street corners the world over. Most people, of course, walk on by, not wishing to consider the state of their souls when so much shopping and catching up is to be done on a tight schedule. Listening skills and nuance put aside for a moment, the outdoors preachers do possess a quality many of us Christians lack: courage.

When I was a first-year campus minister at Bloomsburg University of Pennsylvania, I was spending time on campus with a student leader and good friend named Russ Warner. Making our way across the dorm quad, we saw a massive, heckling crowd gathering. We were struck by the interest in the man at the center of it all: a notorious street preacher who had no qualms about calling out sorority sisters as whores. If he had merely stood on the grass bank inviting weary sinners to find rest in Jesus from their failed attempts to find purpose in their life (or some such caring, inviting message), the students would've just bolted past to class or their dorm rooms. He knew how to grab attention. He stirred up a lot of heat over the evil of the Roman Catholic church and all the fake Christians out there. Russ and I couldn't take it anymore. In turn, we addressed the crowd with the loudest voices we could muster, to get a few lines in. We basically dismissed the preacher as an inadequate representation of Christianity and invited them to look at Scripture for a more loving picture of God. I've never been more courageous or disheartened. As we spoke, the crowd, including the pulpit bully, dispersed. Life went back to its mundane quest for video games and easy A's on quizzes.

Do we have to stand in public, presumably against the wishes of our fellow earthlings, to grab some attention just long enough to jam the Good News in? If not, must we spend fifteen million on a Super Bowl ad with Jesus' name in it to feel like we've fulfilled our commission? Where is courage most needed? We need courage in two areas: in speaking up when serious questions are being asked and shutting up when our words will only create hostility.

Slow to speak, as a general rule of thumb for godly communication, does not imply cowardice. The street preachers do not have a corner on courage. In fact, my sense is that many of them are hiding from the painful, awkward, and sluggish task of honest personal interaction. We Christians need courage to speak up, perhaps even taking the risk of not doing it perfectly. Merely being nice people or even being culturally-creative Christians for the common good (something desperately needed in our land) is never enough. Someone needs to "speak for God," as Charles Colson pleaded for in his book of the same name in the 1990s.

As an example of the powerlessness of cultural Christian forms, consider holidays. Each Christmas and Easter, thousands of otherwise enlightened and affluent Americans join in the tradition of the *Messiah* Sing-in. At the "Hallelujah Chorus," the room rises to its feet in a crescendo, reminiscent of the bout of delirium Handel experienced in composing it. The singers may feel for a moment they've been ushered into the seventh heaven. But when have we seen any breakouts of repentance and heartfelt worship toward the glorified Jesus from such a glorious experience? Any number of Christ-honoring relics in our society have the same effect: another fine moment of human transcendence, perhaps, but no human transformation. Why is this?

It's pretty clear the difference is that we are not created to respond to God merely by His good works in nature or in its human cultivation. We are created to respond to God Himself as a person. He speaks natively, we might say, through creation, but speaks savingly through His Word. This is not to say a mere reading of Scripture will convert someone's soul—assuming the Bible is the Word of God, which I do believe.

What's the missing link? According to the Apostle Paul, the link is proclamation. "How can they believe without a preacher?" Preaching here can mean any kind of human-generated communication of the Gospel. The New Testament uses a plethora of different terms to describe the act of communicating spiritual truth. Everything from arguing, discussing, telling, and speaking falls under proclamation. The common denominator is not how well it's done or who's doing it but that it's getting done. The power is the Gospel itself conveyed by a human voice.

Raised with no biblical literacy, I was first encouraged by my friend Scott to "take up and read" the Gospels of Matthew, Mark, Luke, and John.[4] These readings gave me the raw knowledge of Jesus of Nazareth at that point. In fact, I was drawn to His character convincingly. Still, I had no idea what to do with His words. Not until I met living Christians in my freshmen year at college who, in faltering ways, encouraged me to leave my self-designed assumptions and follow Christ back to God. Somewhere in the span of a month or so, I put my trust in Christ, and that's how I fell into the stream of Christianity. In those early days, I experienced a host of ill-conceived and well-conceived outreaches by Christians. This partly explains why to this day I'm just as committed to human agency in the expansion of Christianity as I am to the supernatural works of God. They work together like the armless man pedaling the tandem bike behind his legless friend steering in the front. They don't go anywhere without each other.

There are many public displays of Christian faith in our world; some are like the *Messiah* sing-in, and some are intentionally meant to turn people to Christ. An altar call at the tail end of a drive-through Christmas Candy Land may be a bit tacky culturally, but it's likely to work. The bottom line is that we need to preach. But we've got to find a way to preach that's not preachy. We can do this by speaking up in a way that is on a bridge and not from atop a wall. We can act as bridge-builders through civility.

When Paul quoted the Epicurean and Stoic philosophers and poets on Mars Hill (Acts 17:16–34), he was showing us one way to speak to a pagan culture. By listening keenly to the heart-currents of his time (and knowing his Bible pretty well), he could construct a bridge of understanding and civility to his hearers. But note, he wasn't aiming at being accepted by the Athenians. He was courageous enough to speak very openly about God as Creator and Jesus as Risen Lord. He held nothing back. But he never quoted Scripture to them. He didn't have to. He not only created a bridge, he walked out on the bridge that was already there: *humanity.* By being quick to listen and slow to speak, he remained faithful to his Lord as well as relevant to his audience. Such bridge-walking takes a lot of effort, but it is mostly an effort of love.

Most of my activity takes place in the small city of Lancaster where over half of the population is nonwhite. College students, retirees, young families, Puerto Ricans, African-Americans, and numerous immigrant communities make up the sixty thousand souls near me. The pervasive culture, however, of my upbringing and Lancaster County is what's called Pennsylvania Dutch. Deriving from German immigrants in the eighteenth century (many Anabaptist), the names Hoover, King, Martin, and Stoltzfus still reign supreme. Not all of us are Amish or Mennonite, but most of us share a Germanic heritage that is felt in our generally reserved, suspiciously friendly, and occasionally dour disposition. It's noticeable to new residents from the gritty and in-your-face cultures of Philadelphia, New York City, and New England. I refer to honest and loud interchanges as "getting Philly" on with someone. The common tendency in a disagreement in Lancaster is to bury feelings, hold grudges, or turn a cold shoulder. Passive aggression is not merely the property of upper Mid-Westerners (with all due respect to Garrison Keillor)!

A nice culture is better in many ways than a violent or contentious one, but it's still merely nice. And "nice" is not a biblical quality. Imagine the Apostle Paul as nice. Kind, perhaps, and self-controlled. But he was far from nice. He got in Peter's face about his racism. He called on the enemies of the Gospel to castrate themselves. He reminded the Roman ship captains, "I told you so," after their shipwreck. As a people, the church must not back down from confronting injustice and whatever else is going on that steals dignity from our neighbors. Let that be our clarion call to speak up. It takes courage to speak the truth in love. Courage will lead us to speak up, and it also enables us to shut up. Both are done in love and for love's sake.

In a religious culture that assumes an audience is either part of your tribe or part of an opposing tribe, I want my friends to walk out on the bridge that God has given us: our commonality as human persons. This is exactly what God did when He "tabernacled" among us in Jesus, and continues to do today whenever we encounter one of His followers who is quick to listen and slow to speak. Numerous speakers have thanked me for the opportunity to use their interests, hobbies, and life practices for the common good. This is one part of curating my forums that excites me.

My daughter Eliza and I share an olfactory sensitivity. We're in good company. The Apostle Paul seems to enjoy odor metaphors as well. He likened the apostolic presence in the world to "the aroma of Christ." To those who were on the road to believing the Good News, he and his friends were the smell of life. To those who wouldn't listen, the smell of death. Speaking truth in love doesn't guarantee a welcoming reception. But it will be a fragrant offering to our Creator. I hope that by His grace, it also will conjure up an ache in our hearers' souls and they'll say, "We've smelt 'the scent to us of a flower we have not found, the echo of a tune we have not heard, news from a country we have never yet visited.'"[5] What ties together quick listening and slow speaking? Goodness, mercy, and patience. Distilling these three, we produce kindness. And kindness is the raw material of civility. Kindness is the elegant bridge we must venture onto with God Himself.

ENDNOTES

1.   Alain de Botton, *The Architecture of Happiness* (New York: Vintage International, 2016) pg. 204.
2.   Frederic Sports, *Hitler and the Power of Aesthetics* (Woodstock & New York: The Overlook Press, 2003).
3.   H. Richard Niebuhr, *Christ and Culture* (New York: Harper and Row, 1996), pg. 40–43.
4.   *Confessions of St. Augustine,* Chapter 7, Christian Classics Ethereal Library, https://www.ccel.org/, Calvin College, 2017.
5.   C.S. Lewis, *Surprised By Joy : The Shape of My Early Life* (London: Geoffrey Bles, 1955).

HOSPITALITY

IN THE FLESH

BUT SOMEHOW THERE IS AN ALCHEMY
AT WORK IN HOUSEHOLDS WHICH TRANSMUTES
THE LEAD OF DUTY AND DRUDGERY INTO GOLD.
IT IS THE ALCHEMY OF LOVE . . .
—Thomas Howard, *Hallowed Be This House*

The first thing you notice about someone's home is its smells. When I was young, I was both fascinated and repulsed by these odors. The Youngs' home featured potpourri mixed with an unfamiliar laundry detergent; The Troutmans' exuded concrete, oil paints, sawdust, and fresh bread. In my seminary days, we often dropped in on the Taylors who were ex-Hippie fashion photographers. Their house put off musty floorboards, garlic, and espresso, with a tinge of photographic gear. The aromas spoke of a certain kind of family culture that went beyond the makeup or behavior of each family. My family homestead in Watsontown smelled like meats cooking, hound dog hair, and ashtrays when I was growing up. I'm quite certain my friends also noticed lightheartedness and comfortable conversation. My friend Miles' Mom worked, his Dad was long gone, and he lived below the poverty line. His place hinted at cat urine and unfinished sheet rock. It was no surprise to me that Miles sometimes hung around my house. On one occasion, my Dad jokingly yelled down the stairs to my hang-out room, "Miles, you down there?" In fact he was, sleeping under my pool table. Discussions about the state of the family tend toward structure and behavior. That is, what *is* a family, and how should its members *behave*? But what about how a family smells? What sort of atmosphere should a family exude? In other words, what is its *culture*?

Of these three building blocks of the family (structure, behavior, and culture) which one matters most?

To engage our world well, we must pay more attention to household culture. If you're single, don't worry, I have you in mind too. I'm using household, conceived broadly, and family culture interchangeably. Family structure expectation has shifted from an emphasis on physical to emotional connection. A Dad, Mom, and kids no longer a family makes. Much of this is due to societal brokenness, and some of it is due to a championing of nontraditional arrangements. Christian morality is considered by many to be archaic at best and harmful at worst. For instance, to deny the expression of homosexual passion is to deny someone their deepest identity. Hence, family structure and behavior are controversial topics whether we like it or not. Household culture, however, is something we can explore and discuss as Christians without being backed into moral and structural corners. If a Christian family culture is even possible, it's worth cultivating. It may very well be viscerally attractive in an age when crossing t's is not in vogue. Perhaps its aroma, if Christlike, is an aroma more pleasing to God than all of our morality and structure combined.

If the Christian household is out to exude anything, it would be *hospitality*. What is it about entering someone's private space that is so powerful? I've heard numerous anecdotes from those who work with international college students; the typical non-American scholar will never see the inside of an American home. It's not that Swedish, Chinese, or Iranian guests necessarily come from overly hospitable cultures. Africans do, so I'm told. Some cultures are simply more private. The American preoccupation with household privacy, then, is disheartening. We can spare the extra time, space, and food. Our pantries are stocked. Our houses are massive compared to most of the rest of the world. And, as we often forget, we are a nation of immigrants from the recent past. But we've learned fierce independence, and it's now part of our DNA. My wife Becky and I often hear from church members or neighbors, "Thank you for opening your home." I'm always struck by the effusiveness of the statements. It's as if opening a home is a big deal. It is. We've come to see our hard-earned piece of the American Dream as a private retreat. What if more of us viewed our abode as an embassy?

Because families dwell in specific places, they create an opportunity for showing who God is in real time on "sacred ground." In Thomas Howard's *Hallowed Be This House,* he flips the "household of God" metaphor on its head. Instead of describing God's work in the world as a house, he reflects theologically on a physical home's various rooms. He presents chapters on the foyer, the dining room, the kitchen, the living room, the bedroom, and even the bathroom. His premise is that humans, made in God's image, design houses that picture what they love most. For instance, the dining room is sacred because it most explicitly pictures "the eucharistic vision." A cow's blood was shed. A corn's husk was pulverized at the mill. "Life from death. The most sacred mysteries, shrouded behind smoke and veils and portals, and laid out there in your cereal bowl."[1] Until I read his book, I never realized how vitally important it is to welcome guests carefully and somewhat formally in our tiny foyer. To attend to their coats, to welcome them to sit in our library. When this is done, even to the kid raising money for his band uniforms, each guest is clothed with dignity. I began to realize how a candlelit dining room signals to a guest, "Let's break bread together. Let's listen to one another. Let's take time. You are worth lavishing beauty on." I started to sense that there's a reason, rooted in God's reality, that sex and toilet are private—not because they're dirty necessarily, but because He too has a sanctuary of holiness where He accepts His sinners and won't put them to shame. We Americans are apt to welcome guests into our living rooms through the garage, stepping over laundry; what happened to our front door and fanfare for the common man? Is no one sacred?

I often joke that Becky cultured me by introducing me to suburban values I missed out on in my small Pennsylvania town. Her family ate dinner at a table and not in front of the TV. They drank wine and put on parties. I don't mean to suggest that family culture is the same as pretension or high society. Rather, family culture is what a family smells like, looks like, tastes like, feels like, and sounds like. We are all *en*-culturated in various ways, usually without noticing it. If culture is simply the worlds we create within the world, then houses hold a world worth caring about. Left to themselves without conscious cultivation, households, even Christian ones, fall prey to the lowest common denominator of worldly influences like apathy, abuse, and tribalism. Culture is something that develops naturally, but who wants to revert back to mere nature? To cultivate is to put elbow grease into nature and create culture for human flourishing.[2]

Some aspects of our American culture are shadows from a Christian cultural presence. For example, Americans are industrious and often generous in times of need. No one would call this a cultural sickness. However, sin is always crouching at the door, so even our greatest assets can be liabilities.

Industry crosses the line into workaholism. Family affection turns into feudal-
ism. Pride of heritage morphs into racism. There are divergent opinions, even
in the church, about family issues as egalitarian versus complementarian
gender roles, whether marriage is between a man and a woman only, or how
many kids are too many and how to school them. So, the question must be
addressed: is there such a thing as a Christian family culture, one that can
be inherited, nurtured, and passed on in faith? I believe there is. I see broad
yet deeply significant contours of family life in the Old and New Testament
Scriptures, which I'd like to commend.

Curiously, three general flavors of literature in the Bible address the three
strands of household:

> **DIDACTIC:** The straightforward teachings that prescribe
> the healthiest **structure** for household life. The five books
> of Moses, the apostolic letters, and the sermons of Jesus
> are generally didactic.

> **KERYGMATIC:** The prophetic preaching aimed at
> moving wills and changing **behaviors**. These are found in
> various exhortations within stories and in sermons of the
> prophets, of Jesus, and of the Apostles.

> **PARACLETIC:** The artful literature that comes alongside our
> human **culture** to offer guidance and sympathy in the broken
> and confusing realities of life. Historical narratives, parables,
> apocryphal visions, poems, and wisdom collections make up this
> type, and they form the majority of the Bible's pages.

The third person of the Trinity, in historical Christian faith, is the Holy
Spirit, translated "the Paraclete" from the Greek. To discover the aroma of a
God-centered household, we are fortunate that much of the Bible is paracletic.
He understands that His image-bearers need much more than rules and regu-
lations. We are wired for relationship with Him, with others, and with our own
selves. We are persons just as He is a divine person.

Ruth is one such story in the Scripture which puts out an alluring aroma of household culture. The human hero of the story is Boaz, a faithful Jew who ran a business threshing grain. Naomi and Ruth, both widows, show up in Bethlehem destitute from living in Moab. Ruth was a Moabitess, but caught the infection of Yahweh worship from Naomi despite how much Naomi complained of her bitterness to God. Eventually, Boaz does more than give Ruth a job and grain. He acts as a Kinsman Redeemer, buying back Naomi's land and marrying Ruth. It's a lovely, romantic tale, of course. But it's ten times more. Boaz "liked" Ruth, but he wasn't acting in self-interest only. A closer kinsman had first dibs on Ruth. That guy wasn't willing to take on the ladies' whole estate, so Ruth became free to wed Boaz. The good guy won. Naomi, as a result, was hooked up once again to her covenant community, and Boaz became the great-grandfather of the one and only King David.

What was the aroma of Boaz (without thinking too literally about his long days in the field)? Boaz was covenantal. He intentionally pursued relationships, lived within God's law, and established a culture, evidently, of deep respect toward women, the land, his extended family, his workers, and Israel (his church). Yahweh Himself, who is only referenced by the characters, operates behind the scenes as divine covenant-keeper. No wonder the book ends with Naomi praying to the same God, the one she also felt comfortable berating in her bitterness. These characters are real, broken, and aspiring people. They are drenched chicks tucked under Yahweh's wings of refuge.[3] They are the ancestors of Jesus of Nazareth. The God of the Bible has no problem drawing straight lines with crooked sticks. In fact, He seems to enjoy it. This covenantal picture carries over into the New Testament words of Ephesians 5, which tell children to obey parents, wives to respect husbands, and husbands to die for the interests of wives. There is no disparity between the values of structure, behavior, and culture in the pages of the Bible. Spliced together, they equal a call to covenant faithfulness under one Creator.

The Row House Forums grew out of our sense that a Christian embassy on College Avenue was much more than presenting a happy husband and wife and their obedient children. If only it were that easy. On the culture front, we tried to set up conditions that would enhance a Christlike aroma. We can't say we succeeded greatly with that, but we do know that hospitality played a big role in our intentionality. Numerous church small groups, parties, and informal hangouts took place in our modest first floor—consisting of a foyer, front room (library), dining room, and living room/kitchen in the rear. Groups tended to spill out onto our front porch or rear patio. Our kids grew up with this, no worse for the wear. Not surprisingly, our forums themselves emerged in this space. I vividly remember Claire Battle finding her place on our steps to listen to a speaker in our dining room. Our "house forums," (as we refer to them now that we've outgrown them) were exciting and cozy. Any more than fifteen participants and they were also a bit chaotic. Sight lines were challenging. Dogs wound between knees with coffee cups balanced on them. Sirens sometimes wailed down College Avenue. Claire, a teenager at the time, may have sat in on Graham Denis's fascinating lecture on "How the English Saved Civilization" or a candlelit interpretive reading of Leo Tolstoy's "Two Old Men." In a promotional video, Claire recalls our forums with fondness. She came our way through our older daughters, who spent a lot of time in others' homes in our neighborhood. Little wonder that I invited Claire to speak as part of our Summer 2015 series. She spoke on "The Poetry of Metamorphosis" and talked about the intersection of and literature. Years later, she and her husband Jon began their own house-held salons, called Chalk Talks.

Just as the three-strand DNA of a household cannot be untwined, neither can a household be understood apart from its physical dwelling. Our family culture is as much influenced by our personalities as it is by the fieldstone, red brick, hardwood planks, plaster, lathe, and slate that make up our row house. The very design of our dwelling has influenced the flavor of our home life. So, in 2011, I threw a hundredth birthday party for our house. Five of our neighbors came in response to a flier I had distributed on our block. One lady came with a bottle of wine and a snack. I had asked a young architect from our church to speak on the evolution of Lancaster City home design. He gave us a great slide show. It struck me again how sturdy, airy, and human-embracing a row house can be. I talked for a few minutes about our own story with this particular house. Since I didn't want to strain the partygoers' indulgence, we sang "Happy Birthday" (as one does to a house) and enjoyed chatting. Later, I wrote this ode to the special place in which we've been privileged to attempt a Christian household culture for the sake of the world:

A TRIBUTE TO 413 COLLEGE AVENUE

Thanks, dear inanimate object, for enclosing a home.

For never moving through the throes of mouth braces,
disappointed dreams and job changes.

For showing off the deep earth in your red clay bricks,
Victorian husbandry in your horsehair plaster, and the
American Dream in your 2000 square feet of family air.

Kudos to the workaday architect who laid out
College Avenue sometime around 1907 and who probably
had a tough time sleeping with the repetitive streetscape
in his mind: Two houses conjoined, up a foot,
and two more separated by thin, arched alleys.

Claustrophobic, dense, mundane? Never. Not with windows placed at
front, rear and side; really, anywhere the designer could cram them.
Our next door neighbors can talk to us by "visual" phone through our
bay windows. Nice touch, sir.

Hurrah to human scale. Approaching our row house is like the
embrace of an old friend or a new one you want to linger with for one
more cup of tea. Verticality in door and windows bespeaks a father or
mother, someone to look up to, to trust,
to be caught up in. And up she goes through narrowing
staircases of carefully-lathed balustrades.

To top it off, many nights were spent with teenagers
on your flat roof watching fireworks, entranced by the city
laid out before us within a canopy of old trees.
It's country up there, the streets muffled and harmless.

Here's to the families who lived here before us.
Of note, Mr. & Mrs. Groff who seemed to be here from 1937
to whenever Mrs. Groff was widowed in the 1980s
(the city directories and deed books are tough to decipher).

Here's to the family who converted the
middle second-floor bedroom into a bath after the Groffs,
a welcome luxury for my family with five women.

Here's to the family just before us who installed a modern kitchen
with elevated counters to match Mrs. Brown's stature (not that we
notice much of a difference except when my belt loops catch on the
drawer knobs). When we first looked at the house, a crayon greeting
made by three-year-old Alex Brown said, "Get better, Daddy," or a
similar sentiment. The wish
was a leftover. His dad had already died of cancer, and
that's how we got you. A family torn and moving on.

We moved in and knew we had our work cut out for us.
That work continues now that the roofs are strong, the
Living Room is the way we like it and most of the rooms are about as
good as they're going to get on our budget.

After five years, I finally finished reconstructing, scraping and painting my favorite room of all: Your front porch.

Here's to a Heavenly Father who dwells in heaven,
makes his home among us in Jesus, and continues to
take notice of His children's needs for shelter. We share this house
because we know it's not our own.

As unique as our domiciles and family makeup are, there are a few ways
we can all respond to the call to the aromatic life.

First, *grab your attention.* We have to pay attention to those in our care. It
starts with our own selves, by stewarding our health and habits. Then it quickly
turns to those nearest us: a spouse, children, and whoever else we care for, such
as foster children, aging parents, tenants, guests, neighbors, or the odd teenager
who ends up sleeping over. We must pursue our achievements and our work subsequent to these commitments. We must ask, what atmosphere are we creating
in our home? Does our workplace and neighborhood provide space for people
to know us and know each other? Downgrading relationships below tasks creates a noticeable aroma of neglect. There really are no neutral smells. We either
remember the sweet and savory, or wish we could forget the stale and repugnant.

Second, *contain the middleman.* Life is increasingly mediated. We live on screens. Social media extends our humanity and opens up channels of two-way communication never before dreamt possible. In a way, we are media. Perhaps social media is an advance in media consumption beyond the days of mere couch potato-ism. But we've become a different kind of potato. Our brains' pleasure centers are becoming more and more attuned to the rush that comes from immediate, shallow, and flattering interaction. Social media, along with the conventional entertainment outlets (which haven't lessened in popularity), retard our attention level for eye contact, quality conversations, and reasoned discourse. We would be wise to create space in our culture for immediate reality. Eugene Peterson calls this aspect of Christian culture a "developed interiority," something that can't be cultivated in a family culture overtaken by screens, noise, abuse, and disintegration. Noise, the demon Screwtape proposes, is the music of hell.[4]

Third, *forget quality time.* When I taught in a school, I had to get used to being in a building eight miles away from my house for seven hours a day. And then I had to prepare and go to bed by ten. That may sound normal to most commuters, but it was an adjustment for me. I had always worked out of our home and Becky homeschooled the kids. I made my own schedule, erratic as it was. It felt as if we spent too much time with each other! But it turns out that the quantity time translated into quality relationships. Boredom, as the scientists are telling us now, is good for children. Who knew? We did. There were times, and there are many now, when I would simply sit in our living room with one of my grown girls for two hours talking about . . . whatever. Much happened in those "chill" moments, as my grown children still remind me. "Quality time" was a prescription for family culture given to us in the 70s and 80s to assuage our consciences over too much activity. How misleading it has been. You can't love someone if you don't know them. You can't know someone unless you're with them. And you can't be with them unless you stop doing something else or include them in what you are doing.

Fourth, *use what you've got.* Single people can lead the way for many of us in this area, as is demonstrated by Wesley Hill's book, *Spiritual Friendship.*[5] Not only is singleness a gift, according to biblical ethics, but our own culture has created more space for singles, it seems, than churches have. If there is a target audience for The Row House Forums, it would have to be those loosely called "young adults." In fact, we attract a mysteriously broad spectrum of people, but my hope is to demonstrate the possibility of Christianity as a life to those who may develop into faithful cultural ambassadors. Single people make up a big chunk of that region on the spectrum. Where twenty- and thirtysomethings often lack wisdom, they tend to be cranked-up with ideas, courage, and creativity. Consider the unfathomable creative output of John Lennon and Paul McCartney, along with their bandmates George and Ringo: all under thirty by 1969.

I wasn't single for very long. In the month I graduated from Bloomsburg University I asked Becky to marry me in a most unromantic way. She said "yes" anyway, in her senior year. We were married in May of 1985, and fifteen months later she wobbled onto a stage at Bloomsburg to receive her graduate degree, great with child. Household life changed fast and furious with us. There's a lot of theology and biblical text to shore up the notion that marriage and family are the expected, typical way God works in and through people. There is a wealth of theology and verses, however, that makes plain it's not for everyone. It wasn't the lot for Jesus, that's for sure. We ought to let that sink in a bit: our Savior was physically unattached. And the apostle Paul pulls no punches in 1 Corinthians 7: he says marriage is a gift, great, fine, OK. But in the same breath he wishes more people were able to enjoy the gift of singleness as he does (7:35). There's nothing fishy or diminished in singleness, at least in the Bible or in the vast swath of church history. To fit into a typical church, however, is tricky. Many congregations cater to families but struggle to market themselves as a household of faith for the widow, the bachelor, or the gender dysphoric. When the apostle Peter speaks of the household of God, he meant the gathering of numerous households into one body. Single households included.

This is precisely where focusing on household culture helps us appreciate singles or whoever else doesn't fit the idyllic mold of family we've become accustomed to. Religious people tend to camp out on structure: what makes a group of people a family or disqualifies it from being a family. Nonreligious people seem to be less concerned with structure and focus on what it means to be a good person in the family or society. These are critical concerns for the church and the maintenance of civil laws that protect human rights. But those discussions tend to become political and polemical. Culture in a household may be a bit more elusive, but without attending to the "aroma" of our earthly habitations, we'll miss out on its explosive power to speak to the broader culture.

ENDNOTES

1. Thomas Howard, *Hallowed Be This House: Finding Signs of Heaven in Your Home* (Medina, WA: Alta Vista College Press, 1976) pg 67–68.
2. Merriam-Webster defines culture as "... a: the integrated pattern of human knowledge, belief, and behavior that depends upon the capacity for learning and transmitting knowledge to succeeding generations b: the customary beliefs, social forms, and material traits of a racial, religious, or social group; also: the characteristic features of everyday existence (as diversions or a way of life) shared by people in a place or time; popular culture, southern culture." Merriam-Webster.com, s.v. "culture," https://www.merriam-webster.com/dictionary/culture (accessed October 19, 2017).
3. Ruth 2:12 ESV
4. C.S. Lewis, *The Screwtape Letters* (New York: HarperCollins, 1942) pg. 113.
5. Wesley Hill, *Spiritual Friendship: Finding Love in the Church as a Celibate Gay Christian* (Grand Rapids, MI: Brazos Press, 2014).

IN THE FAITH

WHEN HE WAS AT TABLE WITH THEM,
HE TOOK THE BREAD AND BLESSED AND BROKE IT
AND GAVE IT TO THEM. AND THEIR EYES WERE OPENED,
AND THEY RECOGNIZED HIM. AND HE VANISHED
FROM THEIR SIGHT. THEY SAID TO EACH OTHER,
"DID NOT OUR HEARTS BURN WITHIN US WHILE
HE TALKED TO US ON THE ROAD, WHILE HE
OPENED TO US THE SCRIPTURES?"

—Luke 24:30-32 ESV

One of my neighbors (whom I'll call Jenn) told me she stopped going to church and never felt happier. She and her husband (let's call him Jim) had attended my church for about a year and had moved on to an upstart congregation in the city. I got the feeling Jim was more into it than she was. Without knowing her inclinations, it seemed she experienced church as some kind of obligation or burden. Otherwise, why would she be so relieved? Where I live in Lancaster County, I see a fair amount of folk who have walked out the back door of religion. There are a lot of wide-open front doors as well. It's a veritable Bible belt. The Pennsylvania Dutch brought with them a largely Anabaptist faith from Germany. Endless expressions abound from all over Christendom. If you've made it this far in the book, you probably know some Christians, visited a worship service, or perhaps investigated the source documents about Jesus for yourself. Heck, you may even be persuaded yourself. My own introduction to church life came after a personal encounter with a friend who was changed by his faith. I also read the accounts of Jesus before I ever encountered a group of His followers. I brought less baggage, I suppose, to my faith than others who grew up in it. The work of The Row House, then, feels like a halfway house for anyone willing to investigate the claims of the faith. In through the out door, in the words of Led Zepplin.

Exiting church life didn't begin with the Baby Boomers (my generation). My parents are a case in point. Unlike my father's parents, Dad and Mom left the Presbyterian Church in their thirties. They had gotten tired of the duplicity they saw in its members and didn't feel the societal pressure to belong as older generations had. It seems that without some sort of compelling reason to attach oneself to a particular church, most people head for the exit for all manner of reasons. The most tragic reasons are sexual abuse, cover-ups of bad actors, and the more soft forms of spiritual abuse such as bullying. Some younger folk get tired of "just believe" answers to their serious questions about sexuality, science, and identity.

But as I tried to show in the previous chapter, religious attachment need not be a chain of blind fools lumbering off the gangplank into oblivion. Boaz, Ruth, and Naomi operated within an assumed context of refuge the Bible calls "covenant." For the Jews, relationships were bound by blood. In fact, in a familiar and civil sense, we are all covenantal. For instance, I'm a Becker until I renounce my lineage, change my name, and move to East Africa. My family name affords me many rights, responsibilities, and blessings. This is why leaving a family under any circumstance is excruciating. In addition, I was born an American. I may not always appreciate my citizenship, but to become non-American would be to renounce my citizenship.

Even within evangelical strongholds like Lancaster, the Midwest, and the deep South, there is a noticeable suspicion of covenantal bodies (visible churches). Add to that, there is a cultural trend away from historical connections toward a self-directed spirituality. The Row House has been for me a way to step into that nexus of repulsion and forgetfulness to demonstrate that Christians should lean into their visibility and historicity. Far from an obstacle to engaging our culture with the Christian story, our penchant for visible expressions and historical creeds are what our neighbors need now more than ever. If only we'll show off our best side.

Vinyl single recordings are what used to be called 45's. You'd find the hit song on Side A, the lesser-known track on Side B. Applications of historic texts act the same way. If our culture is heavily individualistic, like ours is in the

West, we rarely listen to the B-side of an ancient passage. Worse yet, we might not notice that the B-Side should be the A-Side. It's not because it's a better song, but because it's making a primary point, shrouded by our cultural myopia. One of the Apostle Paul's greatest hits rarely gets played on the church airwaves because it's been released to the B-side. I intend to flip the disc. The section is found in Paul's first letter to the Corinthian church, chapter 11. We tend to associate that chapter with the words of institution every minister knows and recites whenever communion is served. "What the Lord passed on to me, I now pass on to you, that on the night He was betrayed . . .." We forget, or perhaps we never realized, that Paul had a beef with their practice of this love feast. In fact, that's why he brought up the subject: they were not waiting for each other in the meal. The rich got there, set up their tables with their sirloin steaks and commenced to chow down. Meanwhile, the poor, with their grocery sacks filled with hot dogs, showed up a bit late. They found all the cool people leaning back and wiping their chins. Paul writes off their meal as unworthy of being called the Lord's Supper. He charges them, therefore, to wait for each other. They should "discern the body" instead of treating the poor with contempt. After all, Christians are one loaf, he argues. Jesus gave His body for all equally so His followers could feed on Him.

The A-Side of this passage emphasizes the need for believers to "examine" themselves to be sure they are worthy to take the meal. Most preachers assume that Paul is advocating individual naval-gazing. That is, believers must come to the table repentant or with some kind of intellectual assent regarding Jesus' body and blood.[1] We therefore make individual confession the A-Side of this chapter. But Paul the Producer is clear: he wants the Corinthian Christians, and by extension we who are believers now, to look beyond our individual selves to those around the table. We should "discern" the body in front of us. Our *horizontal* human relationships are where we discern the body Jesus died for. The body is much more than a single belly button. This household notion, if not emphasized in our churches, leads to something worse than tribalism. It leads to caucusing. Where inclusion, sympathy, and mutual support should reign as a direct and compelling demonstration of our engagement to Christ, we instead look more like a gathering of competing souls. It also leads to disembodiment. What Paul is asserting is that an individual believer can pinch herself in the arm and feel the presence of Christ. She could also pinch everyone else in the room to demonstrate to herself that Jesus is real, *corporeal*. The Supper of our Lord is the pinnacle of meeting with Jesus, not because we simply dine with Him in an invisible, spiritual, vertical way. Rather, it's that He is present to bless the whole throng of hungry and thirsty pilgrims in the room. He's as real as the sour aroma of fresh bread. He's as real as the sweet tingle in the wine. He's as real as the corporeal earthlings throughout the room.

"Can the LORD set a table in the wilderness?" the Psalmist asks. He surely does. He calls it church. We need to flip the disc and make the B-side the A-side. In a society of rugged individualism Jesus cries out: "Come to me, *all* you who are weary, I will give you rest" (Matthew 28:11–12). Simply by being the church in a community we have a halfway house to invite the weary into. Without it, we're lone apologists with no home to return to. Simply being the visible church is our ultimate defense and offense. It's how we proclaim our faith in Christ. It's how we proclaim Him.

"This Row House thing. It's a strong critique of the church, isn't it?" This question from a rogue Professor of Philosophy at a Christian college caught me off guard. I hesitated to reply to the question only because I was saddened by it, and slightly warmed by my own heartfelt response: "No. I can honestly say The Row House is not a critique. I started it as a way to help my church build a bridge to our city. I love and need the church." There's a lot of critique of the institution of the church from those who've tried it, found it wanting, and left it. Even those who are still hanging in there wonder sometimes if it's worth it. Many in the "cultural engagement" or "missional church" businesses seem irritated with the mediocrity of our churches.

I attend Wheatland Presbyterian Church, at the corner of Presidents and Columbia Avenues in Lancaster, Pennsylvania. It's made up of congregants, members, and officers whom I know by face and name. When "the church" gets a bad rap in our culture, it's due to some kind of fault in the life of a congregation or flawed individual Christian—the clearly visible manifestation of the invisible church. This can lead people away from the buildings and into a spirituality that's less messy. This is understandable. Seeking an invisible church to the neglect of a healthy relationship with a living body, though, has its own consequences. Christianity is necessarily institutional. Jesus set it up that way. A person can individually believe, but that faith comes to life and is sustained only in the context of God's corporeal family. As some traditions have said, "There is no salvation apart from the church." An online church, for example, is in a tough place to serve a meal or take communion.

This is why The Row House Forums have a wide open front door and a back door to match. I want people to fall into the allure of our topics and wonderful speakers. I want them to have a great time learning, eating, and connecting with an eclectic group of people. I want them to find their way into the ancient faith. It might be by a visit to my church or a return to the one they've avoided. It might be by having a beer with our speaker with me after a forum. As much as I want to reach unschooled unbelievers like my teenaged self, I also want to keep people in the faith. But I also provide a back door for those who aren't ready. I provide a wide open front door for recovery.

Sadly, many unchurched people and post-church believers devoutly believe the stereotype of church as a haven for the self-righteous. There's been a return to authenticity as a result, which itself slides into easily-detected phoneyism. It's time to deflect the criticism, fairly or unfairly leveled, and engage with our culture through demonstrable hospitality. Our greatest tool in this toolbox is our humanity, not our authenticity. Being present with those in pain, serving meals to the weary, and inviting our neighbors into a full-bodied experience in worship is something we can and must recover. When I work with churches to enhance their cultural engagement, I urge them to look at their own "social apologetic" first. That is, do they love each other? How is that made clear? How must they grow in love? How can they create a healthier, more loving environment within their own four walls first? Once that is in motion, it's also critical to consider what outward apologetic (defense of the faith) is most relevant to their context. As I write, the Benedict Option championed by Rob Dreher is in the spotlight among earnest church people.[2] The basic idea is that church must take care of its own business as a community a lot better than it has been so it can offer life to the world rather than becoming engulfed by it. Some evangelical leaders, like Os Guinness, think this approach is misguided. We still live in a free society, he contends, and ought to keep mixing it up in our culture even if it's messy. My Amish neighbors have conduced their own sort of Benedictine experiment. Unfortunately, these radical Anabaptists have turned so far inward that they have become suspicious, if not cynical, toward the English (their term for the non-Amish). They are trapped in a perennial quagmire of inconsistency within a world of technological progress, Target stores, and politics. The Amish, though, are examples of the power of intentional community in our postmodern world. It seems clear that despite the many respectable ways of the Amish, engagement with their surrounding culture is not one of them. Evangelism, for the Amish, is self-limited to their progeny. Must the church create such a closeted existence in order to reach the world?

Being quiet is not the same as being cloistered. Much of what faith-driven people do in the name of Christ goes unnoticed. And perhaps it should: serving the poor, providing healthcare, and laboring daily in households, schools, or on foreign mission fields. The Row House, for its part, is an enterprise in meta-thinking and intended to be very visible. That is, we want people of all kinds to step back, pull back the curtains, and take a gander at the cultural landscape, asking things like, "What's going on here? What can we do about it? What are we doing wrong?" Our forums traffic in ideas, it's true, but we don't mean to be Platonic, as if the doing of Christianity is less relevant. No, Siree. We wish to do our part in demonstrating that Christianity is not only real, it's the only real way to flourish in God's world. By inviting our neighbors to look at the world of ideas, we're asking them to look at us and the manner in which we are looking. As we look together, we hope to squint with them (in the words of Steve Taylor), to make out on the horizon the arrival of a perfect kingdom.

Leaving the Amish countryside for a moment, I will share a few other examples of intentional cultural engagement being conducted in the realm of ideas, right here in my back yard. I will also offer some kudos and critique, trepidatiously.

1. ST. JAMES EPISCOPAL CHURCH curates a series of Saturday evening masses using respected musicians' compositions as a touchstone for worship. I attended the U2 mass on my birthday and was impressed by the priest's earnestness to connect their transcendent lyrics with the Eucharist while the band incorporated the spirit of their music. Their approach reflects their commitment to leveraging the communion as a tool for evangelism. It also reflects a declaration that all of reality is subsumed under the grander call of humans to worship God. Not a few dropouts from "low" worship experiences have investigated St. James through this front door, a door actually exists in full view of daytime traffic on historic Duke Street in downtown Lancaster. The outreach is unapologetically church-centric and attraction-oriented. That is, the point is to get people closer to Christ by getting them into the sanctuary. I commend them for utilizing popular artists' language without hoodwinking the public or turning art into mere propaganda. My only concern is that it could appear that James Taylor or Radiohead are not worthy of our attention apart from the service of Christ. Actually, their gifts are rooted in creation and can be appreciated at a human level without being leveraged for Christian service.

2. BRIGHTSIDE BAPTIST is also a congregation within our city limits with a rich history of ministry within the African-American population. Besides the expected full array of services on Sunday, Brightside has built and maintains an Opportunity Center. If a white church were to build a similar addition, it might have been called a multipurpose building. But the leaders know it's tougher for people in lower-income households to get a leg up on opportunity. Job training, an in-house bank, and numerous spaces for community-engaged groups were all part of the plan. The black community integrates the various aspects of life more easily than the white population. Voter drives and political meetings are not unheard of in an opportunity center. All of this is meant to put hands and feet on the presence of Christ in the community. It may be tough for such an orientation to remain on task as inner-city populations move "up and out" with advancement, and newer groups, mostly immigrants and refugees, move into the neighborhood.

3. CONVENTIONS are more popular in Lancaster now that our small city has a convention center. One such guest is called the Circuit Riders, born of a triumphalist theology. There are a few other religious conferences that take place in town as well. Inevitably, groups of two and three conferees fan out into the downtown business district to "bring God's kingdom." Conversations about spiritual things are initiated, and people are prayed over. Clearly, this potential for engaging culture, no matter how well-intentioned, planned, or carried out, is programmed to evaporate like a SnapChat post. Worse, they could reinforce the stereotype that Christian communicators need to get the Word out by any means possible, even if it means going cheap on continuity and significant relationships.

4. STREET PREACHERS still exist on Penn's Square during high-traffic events such as First Friday. One particular man with a booming voice caught my eye one day, and I smiled, pointed up to the sky, and said, "Jesus is Lord." I did it to see if it might make him smile, but instead he plowed on about God's judgment for all those who don't repent. I wonder, did he think I was mocking him? I wasn't. These preachers tend to be sold out to their fundamentalist brand: King James Bible, independent, Baptist, fundamentalist theology. For the most part, these men and women isolate themselves and create very little rhetorical traction for Christianity. They reinforce the stereotype of the angry holy huddle. But they do provide a foil

for thoughtful, caring Christians to ask their friends how they react to such belligerence. Spiritual bullying provides a backdrop for humble, modest expressions of faith. For the record, I have known a few Christians to use this method while still inviting crowds, in a gracious and winsome manner, to investigate Jesus. I wish more of those people would come to Lancaster!

5. CHRISTIAN SCHOOLS with open enrollment can provide the deepest and healthiest well of cultural engagement if they choose to do so. I know of several schools that work hard at listening to history and literature in order to integrate their Bible lessons into the real world. That world is sitting in the seats. I venture to say that private religious schools in general do a better job at exposing students to a world of ideas. Public schools, in their reticence to address religions, can only play on the sidelines. In the end, a sustained and relational environment like a school can cultivate Christian ideas and habits. I've seen firsthand, however, that these same schools tend to promise Big Rock Candy Mountain,[3] and end up delivering a decent education that few students really appreciate.

6. PARACHURCH GROUPS, so-called, can also play a part in introducing young people to biblical ideas. I'm a case in point. Not raised within a Christian home, I vividly remember two multimedia shows that came through my public high school at our assemblies. Created by Youth For Christ, they were called *Fat City* and *Love Somebody*. Neither were overtly religious, but each of them exposed an aspect of youth culture in a meta-thinking fashion. *Fat City* dealt with consumption, and *Love Somebody* introduced the idea of getting out of oneself to be a true friend. These assemblies did not change my life immediately, but they cracked open the spiritual parts of me that were completely fallow due to my stoic upbringing. They laid a foundation for a relatively easy acceptance of the authority of the Bible when it was taught to me. They pried open my heart so that a salvation operation on my soul felt necessary. Young Life, through their insanely fun camps, is another organization in public schools worthy of note. At times, these groups unwittingly make the landing strip into the church a bit rough because churches are never quite as creative and fun as a youth gathering.

7. **BUSINESSES.** There are several business in our town that are openly Christ-centered, some going for a wholesome atmosphere, others attempting to do justice. Cafe OneEight is run by an ex-Amish couple who have melded the urban cafe with the agricultural conservatism of their upbringing. One wouldn't know it's a Christian spot except for the occasional worship song over the speakers. The atmosphere is bright, substantial, and safe. My daughter works there with a mixture of Christian and nonbelieving staff, and has appreciated the owner's overall concern for people in the shop. The Sweet Shop, run by Jonathan and Jennie Groff, began their business with a "double bottom line" of profit-making as well as job training for refugee women. Their product—Stroopies—is a rare form of the Dutch stroopwafels found in Europe. And then there's Champ Hall, founder and owner of Champ's Barber School. It's the only place in town I can get a five-dollar haircut. The culture is urban. Meaning I'm one of the few white people in the salon on any give day. Champ is a believer who aspired to "ministry" and found himself making money cutting hair and training a host of at-risk young men and women to do the same. There's nothing overtly spiritual about his shop, but I know Champ's secret. I'm moved, to tears sometimes, when I sit in one of his chairs and watch him mentor his students.

One more word about the church as a means to cultural engagement is *catholicity.* If there is a way we must recover the global and historical nature of the church today, it won't be by pointing to some ephemeral concept of church unity. Perhaps a better approach is to celebrate the church in the historical sense as "catholic." When Francis A. Schaeffer returned from Europe in 1953, he witnessed his own denomination quibbling and bickering over minutiae and acting generally nasty toward outsiders. In Edith Schaeffer's detailed history of the L'Abri movement,[4] she relates how her Fran went into depression. He had to rethink the whole Christianity thing. Here he was, an ordained, Bible-believing Presbyterian minister who was grieved by the lack of charity he saw in his own ranks. When he took two weeks to start from square one, he rediscovered that the clarion call of God in the Bible was for sinners to come to Him, and that the key to His kingdom was love. Schaeffer believed again with multiplied fervor. The fruit of that search was a small treatise called *The Mark of the Christian.* He became enraptured by the notion that God makes His appeal to the world known through the love Christians have for each other. That is, the world will know we are Christians by our love.[5] More radical than that, the world will know Jesus is the Son of God, not by our morality or even by our love for outsiders, but by our love for each other. The power of love sent Schaeffer to the front lines with Christians whom he had before held in suspicion. Linking arms with Roman Catholics, Eastern Orthodox, and Liberal Protestants, those he called "cobelligerents," he ended his life fighting in the public square for the just treatment of women and their unborn children.

If you are a Christian, you are part of the invisible church, Nonetheless, you have to settle for a visible church in order to express your faith in a way that will make a difference with those you love. You can't invite your neighbor to an invisible church. But you can invite him to a visible demonstration of the kingdom of God with all its warts. They enter a threshold and see real people just like them. They can dip their toes into a stream stretching back to the times of Abraham: a mighty river of salvation by grace through faith. They can smell it in the bread, taste it in the wine, hear it in our songs, learn it from our Bible, and feel it in our holy kiss. The church doesn't need to build a bridge to culture. Jesus is the bridge, and we are built into Him. Let us be the church and not be ashamed. Let us engage culture as the only truly transformative household on the block. I started The Row House as an extension both of my own congregation and the church at large. In the best sense of the phrase, I do show off. I do it to pique the interest of my neighbors in the work Christ is doing in His world. I do it as civilly, humanly, hospitably, and creatively as I can.

ENDNOTES

1. Most modern translations of 1 Corinthians 11:29 add "and blood" to "body" in order to tie in with Paul's statement in 11:27 where he uses bread and cup as stand-ins for "body and blood." The ESV, thankfully avoids that error, allowing Paul's emphasis of horizontal relationships within the body of the church to shine: "Whoever, therefore, eats the bread or drinks the cup of the Lord in an unworthy manner will be guilty concerning the body and blood of the Lord. Let a person examine himself, then, and so eat of the bread and drink of the cup. For anyone who eats and drinks without discerning the body eats and drinks judgment on himself."
2. Rod Dreher, *The Benedict Option: A Strategy for Christians in a Post-Christian Nation* (New York: Penguin Random House, 2017).
3. I heard G. Tyler Fischer use this expression about coming to grips with the disparity between the spiritual formation he had hoped his classical school would inculcate in his students and the apprarent outcomes at the time of graduation. He is a devoted fan of the film *Oh Brother, Where Art Thou?*
4. Edith Schaeffer, *The Tapestry: The Life and Times of Francis and Edith Schaeffer* (Waco, Texas: Word Books, 1981).
5. John 13:35 ESV

HUMANITY

EARTHLINGS ARE ENOUGH

WHETHER YOU ARE SICK OR WELL,
LOVELY OR IRREGULAR, THERE COMES A TIME
WHEN IT IS VITALLY IMPORTANT FOR YOUR SPIRITUAL
HEALTH TO DROP YOUR CLOTHES, LOOK IN THE MIRROR,
AND SAY, "HERE I AM. THIS THE BODY-LIKE-NO-
OTHER THAT MY LIFE HAS SHAPED. I LIVE HERE.
THIS IS MY SOUL'S ADDRESS."

—Barbara Brown Taylor, *An Altar in the World*

A photo post on social media caught my eye, of a young man holding out a magnificent freshwater fish. Grasping it by the gill, the hook still fresh in its cheek, the deep green creature's turquoise striping glistened in the sun. In the comments, the fellow wrote, "This fish tasted great even though I felt guilty eating him." His shame was evident, and it broke my heart. After all, harvesting a fish, if done in a way not demeaning to our humanity through exploitation or careless-ness, is something to be enjoyed, right? "I'm embarrassed to be human" is another stock response I hear often to any number of ignorant, foolish, and cruel behav-iors. But just when the world has gone to hell in a hand basket, stories of Good Samaritans renew our hope in humanity. Both mantras echo down through the halls of mass media as well as in chats at the coffee shop: to err is human ... but somewhere deep in all of us is a good heart. The current scientific (largely evo-lutionary) worldview doesn't help us here. On one hand, we're supposed to slow down global climate change. Why? Because we're at the vanguard of evolution and somehow responsible for the earth. On the other hand, we're the ones who love our cheap clothes, gas-guzzling SUVs, and tramp tats. Should we attempt to trump the evolutionary process that will eventually kill off our undesirables, or should we just go with the flow and party on the *Titanic?* If we say we have the answer, are we not being species-ist? It's impossible to find a documentary about the environment that doesn't fall into this hypocrisy: millions of dollars are spent on the highest-tech cameras in order to shoot the living world that is going down the tubes because of our human progress in developing high-tech cameras. We've created a Catch-22 for ourselves: we are human, but we should consider ourselves nothing more than a speck of dust.

Maybe I'm taking our culture's assumptions way too seriously. Do any of us actually live an examined life anyway? René Descartes went down in history for asserting, "I think, therefore I am." Compared to living an unexamined life, living a thoughtful one is better. I wasn't cultivated in my youth to value intellectual rigor, curiosity, and open-mindedness. Without warning, in came a sense of consciousness (and, dare I say, transcendence) during my late teens when I found myself face to face with the person of Jesus. My absorption into Christianity nearly resulted in my turning away, though, thanks to some mildly insane and emotionally immature Christians. Some were Cartesian in their own way: "I feel God, therefore I am." Some overdosed on theology and underachieved in kindness, a sort of Cartesian Christian tribe. But whenever I observed a Christian who was not embarrassed to be fully human and embraced love as their modus operandi, no wonder I heard a ring of truth. Those guiding lights kept me in the fold. One of my treasured human guides lived in Victorian England and might never have touched me if it weren't for my macabre curiosity as a teenager.

I first encountered Joseph Carey Merrick, the Elephant Man, through *Very Special People*, a compendium of human oddities showcasing the stories of extraordinary people, many of whom worked as sideshow freaks. Mr. Merrick was a man deeply convinced that he was made in God's image. In what became a 1980s film trope, Merrick's defense rang out from the Victorian train terminal where he was cornered by cruel onlookers: "I am not an animal! I am a human being!" The director, David Lynch, conjured an eerily realistic film by shooting in black and white and insisting on a realistic reconstruction of Merrick's grossly deformed head and face. In a scene that never fails to move me to tears, Merrick awkwardly stands in his London hospital room, reciting the Twenty-Third Psalm in its entirety—a feat the hospital chairman had thought impossible for such a pathetic, useless imbecile. Merrick believed his worth came not merely from within himself by some strange accident, but from outside himself. Though mirrors were strictly forbidden in his room (for fear of inciting his own despair), he needed to look no further than his own inner self to know, tacitly, he was made in God's image. His mother was a pious Christian who raised him on the Book of Common Prayer and Isaac Watts' hymns. Despite his deformity, abuse, and depression, he loved God, his mother, and himself.

A guiding light these days for cultivating a human spirituality is James K.A. Smith. His book *You Are What You Love* offers a profound summary of the premise of this chapter; namely, that to love is human.[1] We are not merely brains on sticks, pleasure seekers, or independent will centers. Instead, we are complex earthlings. It's no insult to be human because we are made in the image of a God who is Himself a person. We are creatures of habit, motivated by our loves. Only persons can love. Think of it: your image in the mirror is not substantially you. Looking at the human family in all its diversity and individual magnificence, what can we say except that God is necessarily the substance? He's more real, not less, for being unseen.

We need to see again the grandeur of humanity. One of Jesus' closest friends was John. He wrote a theologically reflective account of Jesus' life and teachings. He also wrote three New Testament letters and is most famous for his Apocalypse (the book of Revelation). According to John, Jesus had an impetuous habit of healing the sick. The Jewish fundamentalists of the day preferred he leave the poor in squalor. On one occasion Jesus made the mistake of tying His miracles to His Father in heaven. The religious leaders took issue with Him. Jesus responded, surprisingly, with Psalm 82: "Is it not written in your Law, 'I said, you are gods'? If he called them gods to whom the word of God came—and Scripture cannot be broken—do you say of Him whom the Father consecrated and sent into the world, 'You are blaspheming,' because I said, 'I am the Son of God'?" (John 10:34–36).

"The Jews," as John labels them, dropped the stones they were planning to use for pummeling Him. Now, with renewed vehemence against common sense, they schemed His arrest.

What's strange is that these very Jews were gunners for a messiah. Jesus comes along and does the most Godlike thing in healing a pathetic man, and they react with disgust because He ties His miracles to God working through Him. If they were upset because Jesus acknowledged God, how would they have reacted if He hadn't? Stranger still, Jesus asserts that all people are "gods." Shouldn't the Jews have been flattered? It ought to shake our understanding of human nature that of all people, Jesus (presumably the only Son of God) would speak in such lofty terms about people. He knows humans are fallen. He's looking right at his opponents. But He can't deny their dignity as image-bearers. This is precisely how He's applying the Psalmist's term "gods." It's as if He's saying to His opponents, "Look, I healed this guy with my word. My Father heard my prayers. I'm acting like a son of God, but you can, too. Why didn't you pray for him? And why are you trying to kill me?"

When Jesus looks at people, He doesn't allow their sin to cloud His essential anthropology, which is that we are godlike. But, my, my, how the mighty have fallen. It's so tempting, even for Christians who should know better, to unravel the human and divine natures of humanity. Cleaving the divine and the human is an ancient instinct, governing most cultures in profound ways. Greek thought, culminating in Platonism, calls the material world inherently evil, not inherently good as the Judeo-Christian scriptures affirm. The Bible affirms that humans, though created "very good," are in fact fallen. Evil doesn't exist alone but is always a falling from something good. For this reason, all of us experience brokenness in every area of life; yet none of us are as evil as we could be. A cleanup operation is necessary to rescue our true selves. In this way, we see that there is a split between God and humankind, but the split is not ontological (of our very being) but spiritual. A veil separates us relationally, but by that same veil, torn, a way is opened up to unite us with our heavenly home. Platonic dualism has haunted the church for millennia, evidencing itself lately in the tendency of worship songs to be overly-proccupied with heavenly deliverance from earthly bodies. But Christians aren't the only ones who fall prey to divine/human confusion. Humanists do this by ignoring God completely. Spiritualists put God in His place by creating an upper story for Him and a lower story for us.[2] Polytheists place a gang of gods on a mountain where they act out our human lives on a grander scale. Pantheists call their inner center "god," purportedly deifying humanity while erasing the necessity for a personal God to whom they must answer. But what could be more humanizing than a faith whose main player is a divine human?

What if God dignified the pinnacle of creation, not by extinguishing it but by embodying it?

Christians insist that a divine incarnation took place in the ordinary Jesus of Nazareth. In Him, we witness the Second Adam, the True and Faithful Israel, and the big brother who is not ashamed to call people siblings. "Here am I and the children you have given me," quotes the writer of Hebrews (drawing on Isaiah 8:18). Through The Row House, I've been training a spotlight on the grandeur of God's image, but not by talking about Jesus a lot. I think that's the job of the church as it proclaims in Word and Sacrament Jesus' continuing engagement with the world as He builds up a society of restored people.

We are human. We are earthlings. We bear His image, and we are not to be surprised or insulted by this. I wanted to create The Row House to show off the grander of the cultural mandate given to Adam and Eve, advancing as it is, through those whose very faith in Jesus Christ has drilled them deep into the earth. Our forums give me a chance to show off friends, scholars, and practitioners who are bold enough to side with Jesus and say, "Yes, we are gods with a small G. This is why our work and our ideas and our mission in the world matters. We've been given free reign. We want to glorify God and make the teaching of His Son attractive to everyone. We are the servants of the Savior."

When I worked briefly as a realtor my broker once told me, "Look, Tom. If this deal doesn't work out, no one will die." He said this over the phone while he partied at his house, and I was on the other end landing the plane in my basement. I was new to negotiating deals, and I was frantic. He was right. No one died. The deal went through. In real emergencies, the ones involving our corpo*real* bodies, people do die. Emergency rooms tell the tale. It's the reason we pay handsomely for anything bodily: Surgery, healthy food, and, ironically, burials. No wonder healthcare is in a logjam these days. Our bodies, and hence our cash, *matter* to us as human beings. Christians need not be embarrassed by this any more than they should blush at craving food, love, or purpose. Our Jesus died. In so doing, He dignified toenails, gastric juice, and bones, not only by creating them, but also by saving them from decay. Holy Saturday indeed. Evangelical Christians sometimes sound less like Christians and more like Gnostics. The notions of being free from the body or even "going to heaven" are founded upon a bad theology of creation. God's intention is not to evaporate materiality; His intention is to restore. He loves what He's made.

Recently, Joni Eareckson Tada, a noted speaker and author, celebrated "Fifty Years in a Wheelchair." In one stroke, Joni recognized the limitations of her particular obstacles and her opportunities as a human being. Her paralysis from a swimming accident made her phenomenally influential. At the same time, because she is, like Merrick, a hopeful Christian, she no doubt has some sense that in her afterlife with Christ, she will be renewed in her body. Scripture is opaque about what these new "spiritual" bodies will be like, but we do get a glimpse. The risen Jesus, according to New Testament accounts, appeared very normal and yet seemed to have limitless abilities. My appeal, as a Christian apologist, is not to invite people to an esoteric understanding of the spiritualized self or some such ephemeral enlightenment. Rather, my appeal is to the glorious restoration plan He has put into motion through everyday earthlings. This is why my forum speakers more often than not are everyday people who do normal things and who are hopeful that their work is, in some modest way, a part of God's restoration in Christ.

There are implications for a vigorous embrace of incarnation:

- Church buildings should be designed for human flourishing, not solely for pragmatic body counts.
- Out-of-body experiences should be held in suspicion as less enlightened.
- God-given biology ought to trump our idolatry of impulse and personal preference.
- Genealogies and extended families should contribute to our core identities.
- Doctrines of the church must center on the person of God, especially of Christ, as a fully human/fully God redeemer in history, and not as a mere logical construction.
- Disease, injustice, and disaster are tragedies to be solved regardless of who's affected.
- Corporate worship should be fully human, expressed bodily in singing, standing, speaking, praying, listening, touching, emoting, thinking, healing, laughing, cleansing (Baptism), eating, and drinking (the Lord's Supper).

What's more stunning in the Christian story than the notion that earthlings are personal, godlike creatures is the outrageous portrayal of God Himself as a person. He's a divine person, of course. Nonetheless, He has a mysterious name and a wild personality to match. If you're new to this conception of the Divine Being, I invite you to pick up a Bible and start reading anywhere. This person will surprise, confound, and allure you. But you still may have major issues with this Him.

Taking seriously the person of God as portrayed in the Bible could lead to a deeper faith, but it could also lead you to more questions, skepticism, even agnosticism. That's where it lead an artist I respect and enjoy: Dave Bazan. For sure, I don't know Dave personally; I've only talked with him once. His story is complicated and ongoing.[3] What is interesting to me, though, is that his road to skepticism began by a bold questioning of the plausibility of the Bible's story. He thinks the problem with Christianity is not our brindled history or bad apples (hypocrites, fanatics, ignoramuses). His problem is with the biblical narrative, with Yahweh Himself.

To his credit, he goes toe-to-toe with God himself, not with his flawed followers. Bazan's story highlights a potentially soul-rattling concept: *the God of the Bible is a person you have to deal with*. So, the question is, can God handle our questions? Theodicy, translated from the Greek, means God's justification. That is, how do we reconcile God's actions or non-actions in light of His supposed attributes. You've heard this before: If God is all-powerful, why doesn't He eliminate all evil? When we go down this road of inquiry, we must be careful lest we fall into a self-imposed blindness in reading certain parts of the Bible. We end up looking for internal inconsistencies that may or not be there. We throw out the bath water and don't notice the babies fighting for life. We assign human motives to divine beings. We filter holy actions through our own tainted grids. We fail to take the text seriously. Reading the Bible story cover to cover, we must be careful not to miss a relentless God who pursued an undeserving and clueless people. He walked in the garden, skinned an animal to cover Adam and Eve's shame, provided a host of kings, priests, and prophets to demonstrate His presence, gave them corporeal worship practices that smelled great, and never once demanded child sacrifice (as their neighbors' gods routinely required). Women were always equal in dignity with men, the poor were the noted concern of their communal case laws, and their purpose was to be a light to the nations. The "redeemed" failed miserably at keeping up their end of the bargain. This inborn admission to failure is the number one reason I feel comfortable calling the Bible "God's Word." Who in their right mind would drag their own reputation through the mud? The darkly Jewish, defeated sense of humor doesn't explain the Scripture's arc; rather the arc itself explains their unique contribution to the human experience—and to comedy (e.g., Adam Sandler, Billy Crystal, and the Marx Brothers). In the end, the Bible is a very human book, and that's not something to be ashamed of. In the same way that the church is a human institution where God shows up, the Bible is a very human book over which God has mysteriously superintended. If I weren't convinced of this, I'd have given up my Forums long ago. They are founded upon the conviction that the biblical narrative is not only the best way, but the only way, to understand reality as we know it.

The Row House Forums are meant to be human-friendly. We do that in a few ways: curated personalities, everyday language, magical dialogue, and paired hospitality. I do not take chances often with my speakers. Douglas Davis was recommended to me by a new friend, Andy Long, who immediately grasped my vision for the forums. Douglas was a professor and designer living in Brooklyn whom Andy thought would be a great presenter. Because I trusted Andy (and since all the information I could find out about Douglas made him look legit), I went for it. He was the inaugural speaker of our 2016–2017 season. A "nobody" with an impressive bio, he spoke on "Why Good Design Matters." At least half the room was made up of young folk from the design community. They hung on every word, even the part where he likened the Bible's creation account to a design briefing! FIG Industries, a marketing firm in town that I had a prior relationship with, sponsored the event. As icing on the cake, the event sold out.

I typically know my speakers quite well. That way, I can confidently and enthusiastically promote the event, and feel reasonably sure they will speak to the topic well and bring in some facet of the Christian story that flows naturally. My favorite talk of all was given by one of my closest friends, the artist Matthew Clark, on "The Magic of Harry Potter and Why Alchemy Doesn't Work." His talk was dryly humorous, well-researched, and surprisingly emotive. He showed how J.K. Rowling got to the heart of friendship using the foil of alchemy, a medieval practice she had a firm handle on. The process of refining in Harry's life parallels the sanctification of the Christian who transforms from self-centered to other-centered, even giving his life for his friends.

Besides having an intimate hand in selecting my presenters, I also coach them to speak in everyday language. Not that they can't use technical or academic lingo; I simply want them to translate it. Also, the avoidance of tried-and-true (read: tired) Christian phraseology must be avoided at all costs. A good example of using the bridge of ordinary parlance was a talk given by Dr. Stephen Cooper of Franklin & Marshall College: "Augustine: A Soul in Search of Personhood." Never before has one of our lecturers talked for nearly an hour, keeping the entire audience in rapt attention and desiring more. I had to cut him off. Stephen, though an author and professor at a prestigious college, spoke with clarity, humor, and energy to a diverse crowd on a historical figure of gargantuan proportions. He then proceeded to keep the party going after I turned off the recorder, and we entered the space where the magic happens.

The Question and Answer time after our talks is worth the price of admission. I figure, if any of our podcast listeners really want to experience a Forum, they need to show up for the discussion time. This is where my speakers tend to show their mettle, expertise, and humanness. Typically, a line of one-to-one discussions take place as well after we close the evening. And if any energy is left, a smaller group of us can be found at one of the many pubs within walking distance of our venue in downtown Lancaster. All of this personal time is intentional. I want to demonstrate the power of personal connection on the human bridge between all participants. Pedagogy is the science of learning. We all know that to learn something, say welding, we must grasp the ideas and practice the art. It also helps to watch a journeyman ply his trade (or watch a YouTube video). The more angles at which knowledge enters our consciousness the better. But in the end, one must do it to know it. The Row House Forums are simply my attempt at *doing* apologetics.

I attended a conference in St. Louis on the subject of Christian Courage at my alma mater, Covenant Seminary. The speaker dais was loaded with royalty, and the content of the lectures was top-shelf. Cramming the three main speakers into twenty-four hours, however, felt a bit like trying to swim in a wave pool. On top of that, very little attention was given to atmosphere, meals, or community building. These are the very things that made up the ministries of the people in attendance, many of whom had experienced L'Abri Fellowship, a residential Christian study center. We were instructed to take lunch on our own. So Becky and I hastily invited Ransom Fellowship's Denis and Margie Haack to join us. We drove in separate cars through the bustle of suburban West County to Chick-fil-A where we had a lovely talk. Still, it felt strange. If I were in charge, I'd suggest one less speaker, one communal meal on campus, and some structured play time on the lawn. I'm not a brain on a stick. I'm a human being. My deepest need and desire is to love and be loved in the flesh. The context in which we try to demonstrate the true truth of Christianity is just as critical to our defense as the concepts we want people to embrace.

Besides curating my speakers carefully so as to show off the best humans I know, and leading them to speak to fellow earthlings, and bringing a dynamic sense of interaction to our forums, I insist on pairing the evening's events with the best food and drink possible. And this goes beyond securing the best coffee in town (which happens to be Square One). My team and I look for ways to complement the topic with the refreshments. Here are a few examples:

- Freshly-popped popcorn, lobby candy, and cans of flavored seltzer water at "Hamilton Schmamilton! What's the Big Deal?" with Harry Bleattler of The King's College, New York City.
- Nepalese samosas and pakora with iced coffee at: "Developing-World Answers to First-World Problems" with Chris Horst of HOPE International.
- The Rabbit & Dragonfly Cafe (themed after the British literary

Inklings) hosted "Childlike Wonder in J.R.R. Tolkien and C.S. Lewis" with Matthew Dickerson of Middlebury College.

The more we can do as Christians to embrace our humanity and the personhood of our neighbors, the better. To cater to felt, physical needs is not a lesser ministration than addressing spiritual needs. When I was an undergraduate studying Communications, I met once with a very earthy professor in her office. The physical atmosphere impacted me and has remained indelibly etched in my mind. It has affected my approach to lighting in my home and to how I conduct our forums. Rather than using the fluorescent bank of lights in her cinder block office, she used only floor lamps. By their warm glow, she invited me to sit on a comfortable armchair as she pulled up a humbler chair that was slightly lower than mine. International decor reflecting human expression abounded, and I fully expected to smell incense (perhaps I did). The effect on me was: I'm a little freaked out, but I feel dignified, listened to, and appreciated. This was hospitality at work, speaking to me in a human language too often neglected when we forget that we are created to love and not merely think. The very stumbling block for the Jews and Gentiles of the first century CE confronts us today. According to the Apostle Paul, His own people asked God for a sign.They got a body instead. The Gentiles of his time sought wisdom. They got a man instead. Maybe we want a conquering king. We get a suffering servant. Maybe we want a hip philosopher. We get a life-giver. God became embarrassingly human in the person of Jesus of Nazareth. Like nuclear fusion, the cross of Christ fuses heaven and earth, eliminating the human and divine split in one act. The cross, a moment in history, justifies all who come to Jesus forever. His justification flows into a work of sanctification, superintended by none other than God Himself. His justification is the down payment on a future glorification, and so humans can walk upright. Christians don't need to build a bridge to the world; it's been built. The bridge is humanity. Are we on the bridge?

ENDNOTES

1.   James K.A. Smith, *You Are What You Love: The Spiritual Power of Habit* (Grand Rapids, MI: Brazos Press, 2016).

2.   Francis A. Schaeffer, *The God Who is There* (Downers Grove, IL: InterVarsity Press, 1998).

3.   Stephen Thompson, "David Bazan: Breaking Up with God," NPR.org, October 13, 2009, http://www.npr.org/2011/04/27/113748209/david-bazan-breaking-up-with-god.

NOTHING IS NOT SACRED

AS THERE ARE NO LITTLE PEOPLE IN GOD'S SIGHT,
SO THERE ARE NO LITTLE PLACES. TO BE WHOLLY
COMMITTED TO GOD IN THE PLACE WHERE GOD
WANTS HIM—THIS IS THE CREATURE GLORIFIED.

—Francis A. Schaeffer, *No Little People*

Each June, a fair takes place in Lancaster City. It used to happen directly across the street from our row house. The weather was usually perfect for strolling under the massive trees near Franklin & Marshall College, and the the lawns were swarming with families. Balloons and booths for various activities abounded. Live music played from a stage, and you couldn't really picture a happier group of people. But the event troubled me. My emotions cascade: amusement, despair, disbelief, anger, confusion, and sympathy. As a Christian who loves that God set up families with a purpose for Dads, Moms, and children, the Lancaster Pride Fest always forces a dilemma on me. In my twenty-first-century American skin, I agree that supporters of a homosexual lifestyle have a right to gather, even celebrate. But as a Christian, I find myself awfully conflicted. My gut tells me I would do well to attend the festival, if for no other reason than kindness.

What's kindness got to do with cultural engagement? Nothing, if you're cynical about the world, yourself, or God. Kindness represents an ancient, relational art. It takes us way back, not in time, but in temperament. It is rooted in God Himself, if we're to take the Bible seriously. Perhaps the opposite of kindness is cynicism. Late night comedians traffic in the winking flippancy of "seeing through it all." What began as a quest to actually live like a dog for the man Diogenes in the fourth century BCE wound its way into our day through the European Enlightenment of the seventeenth century. Diogenes, for his part, metaphorically pooped on the higher ideals of Platonism and ran around ragged, moved only by his basest passions. For cynics, revealed wisdom such as Scripture is unnecessary, even dangerous, for understanding our human potential. Christians, though, are often just as cynical toward the world. Instead of weeping over Jerusalem or bearing in their bodies the judgment of others' sins, they sneer. They are tempted to pronounce judgment, a sin worse than those sins they tend to judge.

Cynicism works, though, you have to admit. Vladislav Surkov managed propaganda for Vladimir Putin in Russia from 1999–2011. He was very successful at bolstering Putin's image. According to journalist Sean Cole and a panel of Russian journalists, Surkov did it by creating "an atmosphere where you can never really tell what's true anymore, so everything is suspect." He preempted potential revolts by encouraging the idea that all of life is just a masquerade. The Russians bought it, tired as they were from riding their post-communist, failed-capitalist, oligarchical pirate ship.[1] Exchanging kindness for cynicism, though, drives a wedge between ourselves and our God. It may feel good to dismiss people we believe are living in darkness, but Christian cynicism is the height of tragedy when you consider that "such were some of [us] at one time."[2]

Around the time Diogenes was prancing on the lawn, in 48 CE to be exact, the Apostle Paul was going out on his first missionary journey. A newly minted Jesus-follower, he left Antioch with his pal Barnabas and landed in Lystra, a small town in modern-day Turkey. Usually, he'd hit the synagogue first to speak with the Jews about Jesus the Messiah. There was no Jewish church in Lystra, so he went right to the Gentiles. These were non-Jews, mind you, who also worshiped the Greek pantheon of gods such as Zeus and Hermes. Not only is his kind approach notable as he interacts with these pagans, so also is his message. He basically communicates two things about God that to this day often elude even God's worshipers: He is holy, and He is kind.[3]

Getting these two points across was not a dry Sunday School session for Paul. He felt it deep in his gut. These supernaturalists, upon seeing that Paul and Barnabas had healed a crippled man just by praying for him, rushed in with an ox and laurels. They called them Zeus and Hermes and began to worship them. Notice the urgency in Paul's verbs (*my emphases*):

But when the apostles Barnabas and Paul heard of it, they *tore* their garments and *rushed* out into the crowd, *crying* out, "Men, why are you doing these things? We also are men, of like nature with you, and we bring you good news, that you should turn from these vain things to a living God, who made the heaven and the earth and the sea and all that is in them."

Paul is provoked that these people would worship puny, manlike gods instead of the one God of creation. He is a living God, yet He's set apart from His creation. That's what holiness is. So far, so good. Paul sounds like a typical preacher. But what he does next sets us back on our heels. He declares that God is kind. And not just a Granny-shares-cookies kindness, but in a way that is rarely ever proclaimed even in our churches.

In past generations He allowed all the nations to walk in their own ways. Yet He did not leave Himself without witness, for He did good by giving you rains from heaven and fruitful seasons, satisfying your hearts with food and gladness." Even with these words they scarcely restrained the people from offering sacrifice to them.[4]

We half expect Paul to turn from "God is holy" to "God will judge you." That's not where Paul goes, though. He lays right into a statement that is meant to cut to the hearts of his listeners and drive them to Jesus as the source of their spiritual thirst. He tells them that it is God Himself who gives happiness to all peoples at all times. We have to ask ourselves, are we cynical? Will engaging our world with the holiness and kindness of God satisfy us? Will it make us feel we've gotten the message out? Or must we include a message of judgment? Furthermore, do we even believe that God gives happiness to undeserving, unthankful, and sometimes uncaring human beings? It's a tough pill to swallow. But once you get it down, it gets to work. Apparently, Paul took that pill, and it affected his message and his manner.

C.S. Lewis seems to have had a problem with such "common grace." He says. "God cannot give us happiness and peace apart from himself, because it is not there. There is no such thing."[5] Maybe he was trying to say, "Look, you can't be happy without God." He was wrong and right. Wrong in that the same word for "gladness" is used in chapter two of Acts to describe happiness in God's presence. So, people can be happy and have many blessings from God even if they don't acknowledge Him. This explains the smiles on the faces of folk at the Pride Festival across the street from my house. God is giving them happiness. Why? To lead them to repentance, back to Himself. God is not cruel to be kind, Paul says. He's kind to be kind. That's His holiness at work again. In a sense, then, Lewis was also right: *happiness only comes from God.* Better, then, to acknowledge and love and serve Him than to disregard His blessings. Better to receive His Son Jesus for the forgiveness of sins then to simply trample his blood under our feet. Sin, then, is not equal to "alternative lifestyle;" it is rooted in ingratitude. Unbelief is the worst sin because it is cynicism towards God's blessings and His revealed Word. But if we can believe Paul, our cynicism is no object to Him. He's seen it all before. He sees through us, into our crap, and still heaps the blessings of creation and human experience upon us. Common grace is another way of saying God is merciful. He is kind. As Jesus Himself said,

> You have heard that it was said, "You shall love your neighbor and hate your enemy." But I say to you, Love your enemies and pray for those who persecute you, so that you may be sons of your Father who is in heaven. For he makes his sun rise on the evil and on the good, and sends rain on the just and on the unjust. For if you love those who love you, what reward do you have? Do not even the tax collectors do the same? And if you greet only your brothers, what more are you doing than others? Do not even the Gentiles do the same? You therefore must be perfect, as your heavenly Father is perfect.[6]

On a writing trip to central Florida, I was asked to speak to a youth group in my friend Chris Clark's church. They knew me not from Adam, but I'm quite comfortable being set before sixty or so sixth- to twelfth-grade students. I came armed with the passage I just described, and a few stories from my youthful past. The response I received to my Oldsmobile 442 story disturbed me, though. I recounted the episode in which my Dad allowed me to drive to a neighboring town in the aforementioned show car. He gave me one condition: "Don't race it." Did I mention it was a 1967 convertible with a 350 cubic inch V8 and 400 horsepower? You bet I did. My two best mates, Tom Troutman and Miles Wilson, were with me in the white vinyl seats. We pulled up to a red light, stopped, and glanced to our left. Three rather unkempt dudes in a beat-up pickup revved their lackluster motor, taunting us to race. Green light. I punched the accelerator, and the Olds lifted like a speedboat. I dropped it into second gear and immediately let off the gas, allowing the muscle car to coast to a responsible speed. The yahoos rushed by us, laughing. At that moment in

the youth meeting, I asked the crowd, "Why do you think I backed off so suddenly?" I wasn't surprised by their answers: everything from fear of my Dad
punishing me to my desire for future driving privileges to avoidance of arrest.
I assured them that wasn't the reason, essentially. None of them came close
to what I was actually feeling. What stopped me from racing was a dash of
all those lesser motivations, for sure, but the real reason was Dad's kindness.
Was he nuts for allowing his seventeen-year-old son get behind the wheel of
such a ravenous, rolling machine? Maybe. But more than that, he was being
kind, generous, and merciful. When I told the kids my deeper motivation, it
was as if none of them experienced parental kindness as a factor for doing
anything. For them, life was to be lived out of legality, shame, and the fear of
consequences. Truly, I was sad to think that perhaps Christians, of all people,
are raising up a generation of culture engagers who are not liberated by God's
grace and mercy. In other words, if we really believed sugar attracts more
bees, why are we spraying our households with vinegar? It's no different in
our approach to the culture around us. To engage our culture well we must be
perfect as God is perfect (holy). And how is His perfection displayed, according
to the Great Teacher? Through His kindness.

For that reason, I've attempted to create events that are unashamedly
Christian in their moorings, but intentionally positioned for the common good.
If someone comes to a forum like "Gaming is Serious Business" featuring my
friend Trip Beans, and they learn something, eat a great cupcake, and get their
few dollars' worth of enjoyment, I've succeeded. If another guest hears for the
first time that God is a divine "player" who made us for joy and happiness,
and that same person can't get that thought out of their head the next time
they're alone in a hotel room wondering if their life matters, I've succeeded. If
one my forums creates an arena where a convinced Christian listens to and
and learns from an agnostic on any point of the human experience, I've suc-
ceed. The bridge to our culture has been built; it is our shared personhood.
When we add kindness to the mix, we create an elegant bridge where freight
smoothly migrates back and forth across the chasm between "us and them"
and between us and our God.

This common grace understanding has led some to formulate ways of
ensuring we don't lose our Christian voice "wherever the curse is found."
In the early 1890s Abraham Kuyper gave The Stone Lectures at Princeton
Seminary. In book form, his reflections are known as *Lectures in Calvinism*.
Though Calvin is mostly known as the predestination guy in the church and

by the "Calvinist work ethic" in popular understanding, he was actually a cultural reformer. Having been pressed into service in Geneva where he led a Reformed renaissance, he laid the groundwork for revivalists like Kuyper in the late nineteenth century. These days, authors such as Craig Bartholomew, Richard Mouw, and James K. A. Smith, though technically advancing the Calvinist worldview, are unashamed disciples of Kuyper. Father Abraham expanded and deepened the Calvinist view of life in which "there is not one square inch over which Jesus Christ does not say, 'Mine!'"[7] When I say a Calvinist vision undergirds all I do at The Row House, it is this world-embracing, broad view of all of reality I'm camping out on, and not just the so-called doctrines of salvation. The major contribution to cultural engagement that guides my choice of topics is Kuyper's notion of "sphere sovereignty." Ably described by many others more versed than me,[8] imagine a large circle called the Kingdom of God. God reigns over it, of course. Within that circle you see other major circles: civil governments, the family, education, business, and the church (the amount of spheres is up for debate). Each of these smaller circles interpenetrate each other to different degrees. But the key to this Calvinistic scheme is this: each sphere has its own sovereignty and way of doing things, even though they have to collaborate with each other well. What's even more significant is God's role: He owns them all and cares for them all, having created each one with its own integrity. For instance, there's no need for a national, civil church. The church ought to be free, but it ought also to serve as a prophet to governments without telling them how to operate, per se. It goes the other way, too. The state must not control the church, but it must protect it and prosecute those who do evil.

A current example of this approach to cultural engagement that doesn't leave any part of reality outside the purview of Christ's intentions is the "Channels of Influence" used by Gabe Lyons and his organization Q Ideas. In order to encourage Christian involvement across the entire human experience, they curate dialogue on seven streams of society: Church, Social Sector, Business, Arts & Entertainment, Education, Media, and Government. Sounds very Kuyperian to me. In Lyons' manfiesto for Christian cultural involvement, *The Next Christians*, he informs his readers that in the 80s, a very savvy and intentional gathering of gay activitists gathered to consider how they might influence similar veins of society in America. Decades later, is there any area of our culture where homosexuality is not positively referenced or positioned? His seven channels are taken from the same playbook but with a different motivation: we Christians are not out to gain acceptance and cultural ascendency. Rather, we want to faithfully serve our Lord and introduce human flourishing to all people for His glory.

People often ask how I come up with speakers for my forums. I tell them I'm interested in everything under the sun and I know lots of people I want to show off. They inhabit the holiness and kindness of God as they think, write, or practice their various vocations. So, the list stretches off beyond my earthly body's ability to put them in the calendar. To narrow things down a bit, though, I've come up with my own eight theaters of expression I wish to engage in Lancaster. They are derived, I've found over my lifetime, from three things: first, I want to elevate my city's cultural conversation with a talk such as "Debt, Greed, and the Common Good," an exposé of how banking actually works on a macro level. Second, I want to lean into the common concerns of Lancastrian's as when I hosted a conversation on "Welcoming the Stranger: Immigration and Refugees in Lancaster." That event took place days after a federal election that highlighted the plight of new citizens in our country. Third, my personal proclivities and pet concerns make The Row House particularly "Thomastic," and I think that gives The Row House a unique feel. Why else would I book myself to talk on "Human Oddities and Lady Gaga's Little Monsters" or invite filmmaker and musician Steve Taylor to speak on "The Art of Courage." I cycle through these eight theaters of expression when I plan out my forums:

THE BUILT ENVIRONMENT: *Town design, community life, transit, sustainable technology*

CLASSIC LITERATURE: *Great books from ancient to medieval to modern and current*

ART AND DESIGN: *Visual language and beauty in its history and current expression*

CULTURAL ENGAGEMENT: *Approaches to understanding and living in our world*

HEALTH: *Mental, emotional, and physical*

JUSTICE AND MERCY: *helping without hurting, economics, reconciliation*

POP CULTURE: *Media, popular arts, consumption, creativity, entertainment*

WONDER: *fiction, whimsy, imagination, joy*

Our season lasts from September through May, giving me eight slots to fill, and as I said already, I probably should be curating a weekly event with all the ideas and contacts I have!

In Maplewood, Missouri, an ambitious pastor wanted his church to make an impact where his community felt most hopeless. His team approached the high school principal and asked, "What do you need help with?" The administrator admitted she could not find a solution to a growing number of kids who came to school tired, hungry, and unable to concentrate. If they came to school at all. The reason? No household in which to get a good night's sleep. So, the church prayed and thought about it. They came up with *Joe's Place*: a residence for at-risk teens where they can live stably and comfortably for the week. The church purchased a property and hired a young couple as houseparents. Today, Joe's Place has enabled dozens of students to complete high school without the distractions of an impoverished home life. At the same time, Joe's Place doesn't remove the kids completely from their families. Imagine the needed conversations that are hatched between everyday church volunteers and these kids' families. Conversation, it turns out, is a precious commodity for kids like these. I can imagine many "intentionally unintended" consequences such as job searches, recreation, and vacations bubbling up out of Joe's Place, all because some Christians were willing to ask, "What do you need help with?"

There is a regrettable impulse in each of us that wants to rain on others' parades. We don't want people who are different from us to have too much fun. This is precisely where we must learn God's kindness. I was struck by two radically different interpretations of the rain that fell the day Donald J. Trump was inaugurated President on January 20, 2017:

- Franklin Graham: "Mr. President, in the Bible, rain is a sign of God's blessing. And it started to rain, Mr. President, when you came to the platform."
- *The Guardian*: "Even the heavens wept as Donald Trump stepped forward to become America's 45th president."

I've read those quotes aloud to several audiences, and they always produce hearty, if not nervous, laughter. I hope you picked up on the humor. The God of creation sits enthroned and laughs, too. And then He mercifully showers his whole, beloved creation with rays of light and downpours of water.

Why? Why not? He is holy, and He his kind. We can't out-kind Him, but we can learn his mercy, and it will remind us that nothing is not sacred.

Which begs the question, "When is the God of the Bible just? Is He ever cruel to be kind, as the axiom goes?" Actually, yes, He is. Like a rainbow spanning the sky, His bow is directed back at Himself. The piercing arrows of His holiness were directed to heaven so He could smile upon His earth. Isaiah 53 says it was "God's will to crush Him," speaking of Jesus the Messiah. He has turned His own wrath back upon Himself by becoming one of us, fulfilling the righteousness we failed to live, and dying a death we deserved to die. This is the savior that Paul was attempting to bring to this crowd who worshiped their puny, selfish, powerless Greek gods. We sinners, including Christians, are never an object for Him; rather, we become the objects of His mercy when we put our trust in Him.

We need this message of insane kindness today. We need to be transformed by it more than ever if we call ourselves Christians. God, wonder of wonders, is even kind to us who don't do a very good job of representing Him to our neighbors. May He transform us to be more like Him: Holy and kind.

ENDNOTES

1. "The Other Mr. President," This American Life, (April 14, 2007). https://www.thisamericanlife.org/radio-archives/episode/614/transcript.
2. 1 Corinthians 6 (ESV).
3. Acts 14:8–18 (ESV).
4. Acts 14:16–18 (ESV).
5. C.S Lewis, *Mere Christianity* (New York: HarperCollins, 1952).
6. Matthew 5:43–48 (ESV).
7. *Abraham Kuyper: A Centennial Reader,* ed. James D. Bratt (Eerdmans, 1998), 488
8. James K.A. Smith, "The Reformed (Transformationist) View," in Five Views of the Church and Politics, ed. Amy E. Black (Grand Rapids, MI: Zondervan, 2015). Smith cogently and creatively describes the Reformed view of political involvement, showcasing the sphere sovereignty approach against the backdrop of four other views: Anabaptist, Roman Catholic, Black Church, and Lutheran.

LOVE THE ONE YOU'RE WITH

MAYBE TOMORROW WHEN HE LOOKS DOWN
ON EVERY GREEN FIELD AND EVERY TOWN
ALL OF HIS CHILDREN AND EVERY NATION
THERE'LL BE PEACE AND GOOD, BROTHERHOOD
CRYSTAL BLUE PERSUASION.

—Eddie Morley Gray, Mike Vale, and
Tommy James, "Crystal Blue Persuasion"

As recently as 1950, most Americans lived provincially. That is, a person could expect to grow up, raise a family, work, worship, and engage in civic life within a few square miles. Commuting as we know it today was impossible because the interstate highway system had not been initiated. Outlying areas were populated by farming families, adventurers, or modern ascetics. Even off the farm, life was agricultural: rooting, shooting, and fruiting was simply what one did in one place for an entire lifetime. Cities were more obviously race-divided, but the populations couldn't help rubbing shoulders. Job transfers were rare, as was air travel. Shopping and socializing largely took place in towns where a person could just about walk to any spot of interest. Trains were busy, shuttling folk from town to town, and in big cities one could get around on subways. It's common knowledge that everything changed after WWII. The Baby Boom was also a boom of car-driven development, heralded by all. Nowadays, many of us feel unsettled. Younger populations are taking worldwide pilgrimages in search of ideal experiences. And when they come back to the U.S., they tend to settle in dense cities where their thirst for diverse experiences can be slaked. Mom and Dad's suburban dream is a waking nightmare of blandness.

All of us entertain fantasies of our ideal life setting. Let me tell you about one of my favorites: *The Dartt Carriage Works*. I imagine myself kicking back with a drink in the firehouse where Tennessee Steinmetz tended to the car in *Herbie the Love Bug*. There I am, working on my fully-restored 1991 VW Weekender Vanagon. Beyond the car bay and living room furniture lies the kitchen, equipped with a brick pizza oven. Gazing around, I see my extensive library, a few finely curated neon signs, some overstuffed furniture, and a thoroughly integrated video/audio system. Upstairs I find the private living quarters: an office, several bedrooms, and a roof garden. At a moment's notice, I'm off to travel the country in my van. It's not like I'm being selfish. The point behind this idea is to host parties and welcome a stream of guests through the wide open front doors. I'm easily reminded that besides not being wealthy enough to create such a joint, I also haven't taken into consideration the exact place it should exist and whether or not neighbors even matter. Furthermore, when I talk like this (and it's often), Becky gently asks me, "Honey, where do I fit into this?" Oh, yeah. That, too. So, that's my dream. What is yours?

What I've come to appreciate over the years is that, thanks to this little thing called incarnation, none of us can have it all. We can't be in two places at once, at least corporeally. We can either embrace this gift from God, or we can fight it. We can receive the gift of emplacement and learn to "love the one you're with," as the hippie song goes, or we can spread ourselves thin as Marmite on toast. We can pretend we live a rich life constantly fueling our quest for novelty, domination, and tranquility. Or we can take up the pot of gold at our feet. We all feel, in some way, displaced, discontented, or disheartened by our place in the world. At the root, I believe this is part of what it means to be fallen. We're "deprived on account of being depraved," to flip the *West Side Story* line. Life east of Eden will never be what we want it to be. The longing for eternal wholeness is lodged in our hearts, but as the Preacher says, we can't find it out.[1]

I've tried to find out what's in my own heart by looking back on where I'm from. My paternal grandparents left Wellsboro, Pennsylvania in the late 1920s to establish a general store in my hometown of Watsontown. It was a booming place up through the 1960s thanks to the steam from the lumbering boom of the late 1800s. Its nearness to Route 80 and a vibrant Philco appliance factory kept the place hopping until the latter closed in 1970. Neither my dad nor Kenny (as my grandfather preferred to be called) ever applied for a job, changed careers, or received a transfer. They ran a five-and-dime, the precursor to the dollar store. Kenny was on the bank board, Dad was a Lion's Club member, and Mom went to "card club" each Thursday night to smoke cigarettes and actually play cards with other housewives. My parents still live on the hill overlooking Main Street, its spires piercing the green backdrop that frames the Susquehanna river valley. My brother Jim lives next door in the house my dad grew up in. I flew the coop to live two hours away in the big, bustling city of Lancaster, while my brother Dave lives a mere forty-five minutes away, deep in the woods of central Pennsylvania. So even in my provincial upbringing, due to economic forces beyond our control, we've found ourselves slightly scattered. Thanks to "growth," my parents' much-beloved store (the one they took over from Kenny) had to shutter its doors in 1986 due to declining sales. Today, Watsontown languishes along with thousands of small towns throughout the country. Ten miles south, another town, Lewisburg, flourishes due to a lot of intentional imagination. It helps that they also have two world-class institutions at their doorstep: the Federal Penitentiary and, more importantly, Bucknell University.

Watsontown is adrift. But closer to a metropolitan region, it might be healthier. The triple shift in scale from horse-and-buggy to train to automobile is most apparent in places such as the Main Line towns of Philadelphia, for instance. They are new enough to accommodate cars, yet old enough to be connected to the big city by train. Places like Wayne or Paoli are still walkable, quaint, and prosperous. But since the late 1950s, the automobile has been the dominant people mover. Our experience of scale, space, and what's possible has dramatically expanded. And though I welcome the future of driver-assisted vehicles, no one knows how they will impact our relationship to space. Any one of you reading this may go to work thirty minutes away. If you live in Atlanta, more like one and a half hours. Your church is twenty minutes away, and the closest place to get milk requires a thirty-minute commitment due to traffic and red lights. Home, then, becomes an integration point, we hope, from the disintegration our postmodern bodies experience out in the wilds of development. Most Americans now live in what is known in the planning community as single-use zoned environments. Commerce, industry, entertainment, and education, we've come to assume, are better served in exclusive spheres. These choices are driven by many values I don't have time to indulge, and other luminaries have written at length on a theology of place. I've particularly appreciated Eric Jacobsen's *Sidewalks in the Kingdom*[2] and *The Space Between*[3] as well as Craig Bartholomew's *Where Mortals Dwell.*[4]

In a world of physical disintegration, I founded The Row House to demonstrate integration of life. For me, the easiest way to achieve that was to go back to my small town roots and live like myself. I also made a conscious choice to center our events in our home or within the limits of Lancaster City. Just so you know, I don't intend to convince you to live in a city. Rather, I simply want to discuss what it means to look at "space" and "place" philosophically. It's something we often don't think about. Jellyfish think about water about as much as you and I think about the air we breathe. So it's helpful to step back to examine what sort of built environment we find ourselves in and to explore its relative merits for engaging our culture.

On one level our choice to focus on town culture was counterintuitive, perhaps even foolhardy, to some. Taxes are higher and crime rates are higher. A half million people live in Lancaster County, while only sixty thousand live in the city proper. A critical mass of evangelical Christians live in the county, making it possible, for instance, to sustain two Christian radio stations. In my own denomination, which is by far not as prevalent as Anabaptist groups, our mother church boasts twelve hundred members. Though we chose to move into a row house in the West End of Lancaster we knew what we were getting into. Lancaster felt more like a small town to me. It afforded great opportunity for our kids to walk, to work, and to gain independence. Plus, diversity, in our estimation, seemed interesting, if challenging in a welcome way. Less Christians live here proportionally, at least the white middle-class types. Many Pentecostal Hispanics and African-American believers live in town, as do a myriad of immigrant groups such as the Bhutanese and Nepali, many of whom are Christians.

In an interview with philosopher James K.A. Smith, Tim Keller speaks candidly about why Christians are, in fact, moving into cities, reversing the "white flight" of the late twentieth century that mirrored suburban development. He gives three reasons: *opportunity, justice,* and *culture.* I will boldly add another reason to Father Tim's three.

By *opportunity* he means that demographics should concern the church. He cites Al Mohler: "If the church doesn't go where the people are, they'll wake up one Sunday without an audience." By *justice* he means that the church should care about the intense problems our cities face, such as economic disadvantage, domestic violence, and corruption, just to name a few injustices. By *culture* he means that cities are places where Christians can have cultural influence. In the arts, entertainment, finance, and politics, the church can set up shop right across the street. As a fringe benefit, Christians can enjoy myriad amenities like walkability, hip "third places" like coffee shops, and the aura of urbanity.

So, I ask myself, why did I intentionally foist the city of Lancaster upon my family in 1999?

I could've settled us in quasi-Amish land where there's more room and less taxes. And the air is definitely more "natural." Was it for evangelistic *opportunity*? Well, sort of. I came to Lancaster to join a near-city church and start a campus ministry. Our house is right next to F&M College. Turns out, I was directed to conduct my work at Millersville University. But my heart was always city-leaning. I wanted to "reach out," but I soon found it's hard enough just being a dad, a good neighbor, and a church member. That is to say, if we had any pretense of bringing people to Jesus, we sobered up quick and found we desperately needed a community to do that. So we've stuck with our church, and through The Row House, Inc., we've made modest inroads into others' lives. But it's been no tent revival. Did we move in to do *justice*? Not really. Christians in Lancaster are already doing many restorative works, and I do what I can to support them. Yet I can't honestly say I've ever been drawn to romantic visions of serving the poor, and living here has only docked down whatever naiveté I moved in with. It takes a lot of faith and energy simply to serve my own household. Perhaps in some way we've contributed to the *shalom* of our place just by being here, paying taxes, and praying. I hope so. What about the *culture*? Now we're getting somewhere. I walk to live music gigs. I go to fancy parties, sometimes on roofs! And, of course, I'm that guy who deserves the best coffee and appreciates urban male fashion. I draw the line at beard oil. I don't even have a beard. In all seriousness, being in the city turned out to be a wise decision financially, something we hadn't anticipated. Our property value has nearly tripled as a result of solid development in the West End. I like that a lot. As far as cultural influence goes, it's impossible to measure, but I do know that living this urban life has been invigorating.

I'm not fully satisfied, however, with Keller's three observations. Maybe it's the assumption that Christians have to be powered by an agenda that fits me poorly: to save souls or to meet needs or to have influence. Maybe I came here with a smattering of all three reasons, but after many years, they simply won't *keep* me here. Here's where I offer a fourth reason for Christians to return to our cities and towns: *people.* Towns are gardens with people in them. As a metaphor for humans, there is no better stand-in than trees. Lancaster is designated a "Tree City." The End (the *eschaton* of all things) will consummate in a garden city so glorious, none of us could fathom its perfection. Why can't Christians live in places for the basic reason that places matter, *period*? I think we can and should. Not for opportunity, justice, or culture alone. Places are not stuff. They are not like things we own, use, or live. We count things worthy because of what they can do for us or what we can do with them. At the core, places are habitation for people. They are a gift from the Creator. No agenda is necessary to complete our Christian calling to our places any more than we need to explain why a tree is a wonderful piece of His handiwork.

When my family moved into our row home, I had a hunch that neighborhood life would give my family a taste of heaven by its very structure. It's happened. God's goodness, beauty, and truth has been experienced in the spaces between the buildings and in the proximity of friends, despite the attendant troubles of our lives. Keller's observations are all good. But before any of these reasons lead to an ushering in of God's kingdom, Christians must appreciate their habitats for what they are and what they point to by their very nature. We can't ignore the reality that cities and towns are loaded with God's image-bearers, prefiguring the destiny of every Christian. For us, to be in a neighborhood has been a way to rehearse God's restorative story for all of humanity.

A few of my favorite words, for some reason, begin with "sp." *Spell, spectacle,* and *splice.* The last one, though, is tops on my list. I came at *splice* in two very different ways. First, as a young hobbyist soldering speaker wires together on my mobile sound system, I encountered splicing at my fingertips. To this day the rising aroma of melting tin and copper from the red-hot tip of a soldering gun speaks to me of alchemical possibilities and memories of my high school sound system. Those are good memories, mind you. I wager that most of us equate splice with slice. Slicing, for sure, is often the first step in splicing. To solder two wires together, I must first cut back their insulation and slice them to size. The end result, then, is not to separate but to join, to twine, to bring together. And this leads to the second way I came to *splice.*

I became a student of the Bible informally when I was seventeen years old. But it took about fifteen years to begin to appreciate the overarching narrative from cover to cover. The story is a universal splice. The entirety of Scripture, some say, is a grand love story, echoed in a chorus you will find throughout its pages: *I will be your God, and you will be my people.* Right up through the New Testament, God is building a city that is distinct from the city of Man. We have Augustine of Hippo from the third century to thank for the picture of a Master

Weaver preparing a bride for Himself out of the tapestry of nations.[5] After humankind is expelled from their garden paradise, a renewal project gets underway with Yahweh acting as architect, builder, and project manager. He keeps up His end of the project despite the resistance He faces from His laborers on the ground. Times grow dark, prophets cry out, the city of Man seems to kidnap the bride completely, and just when history is at its brink, a smoldering of light dawns. This light, a mere person untouched by the inner compulsion of sin, incarnates the bridegroom role. He could've been snuffed out in death on a cruel Roman tree of torture, but instead a *eu*catastrophy ensues. Like the eagles rescuing the outnumbered and beleaguered fellowship of the Ring, morning dawns and the tide of battle was turned, forever changing the course of history and all of Reality itself.

Gene splicing sounds scary, especially if performed by a mad scientist for nefarious purposes. But in the right hands, gene therapy is a laboratory alchemy that gives rise to many wonderful remedies. The Bible is a wild, wonderful, and moving picture of God's hands, slicing and splicing His creation back to perfection. As Cockburn sings, "All you can do is praise the razor for the fineness of the slash, till the rose above the sky opens and the light behind the sun takes all."[6]

As Paul told the Romans who were living under a pompous yet fragile empire, "God will soon crush Satan under your feet."[7] That evil personality has indeed been crushed by Christ so that we who serve Him in fact trample on his dust, if only we could believe it. If we did we might not be so quick to regard the enemies of our faith with anything more than amusement. We might, instead, entrust ourselves to Him who reigns and get on with the business of His kingdom in the exact places we find ourselves.

After Acts 28 (the historical end of the New Testament) comes the posthumous chapter Acts 29, the ongoing history of Christ's church. If we believe the Scriptures, we know that the fuel for such a movement in our world is His very Spirit. And what's the end goal? A mere rescue of souls up into an ephemeral heaven? Hardly. If the GPS called John's Apocalypse is accurate, we can expect something even greater than a throwback to Paradise lost. Earthlings can expect a new heavens and new earth that awaits those who have come in Christ through the tribulation called life on earth. More than that, a wedding reception awaits. A wedding of heaven and earth, of God and His people. This splice will not disintegrate our bodies from our souls but will reintegrate them in the resurrection. Our personalities will not dissolve into God's; rather, He will celebrate our creation and include us in His everlasting, personal project of rest. "[N]o eye has seen, nor ear heard, nor the heart of man imagined, what God has prepared for those who love him"[8] If our future is integration, why should we not strive for integrated lives here and now? Might acquiescing to the half-life of a disintegrated life only prepare us for disappointment in our declining years? Might the effort of integrating our life wherever possible around His cross create better opportunities for knowing ourselves better? Knowing our neighbors better? Knowing God better?

The Row House was founded sometime in 2010 but the vision stretched back to 1982. A single photograph led to my life's work. It was a small black-and-white picture of an English manor house on an expansive lawn of grass. It spoke to me of home and the importance of place, space, and relationships. Like a tightrope wire stretched forward throughout my adult life, the vision invited me to the prospect of creating space, either real or virtual, either sporadically or continually, for intimacy between people. The Row House became an experiment in creating that space, be it ever so small, that might in God's speed become a movement.

I toyed with some embarrassing names for my new work, such as *BECKERVOX* and *EXAMEN*. Thankfully, no one liked them. My intuitive wife turned to me one evening in our row home and suggested, "Why don't you call it *The Row House*?" That was an epiphany. The name communicated the domestic comfort we had enjoyed for over ten years. It easily connected my passion for place with our small city's most common form of residential architecture. It provided me with branding language for turning our chaotic household into a resting spot on the bridge between faith and culture. I then got busy securing a web domain, writing a vision and mission statement, and recruiting a nascent board. We began a bimonthly lecture series in our first floor, which we called The Row House Forum. We served the best coffee we could find, comforting snacks, and sometimes wine and beer. Folks milled around for about four hours on most of those weekend evenings. The idea for our ersatz salons was born the day I laid my eyes on that photo of the English manor.

I was working as a reluctant camp counselor in the summer of 1982 in Ligonier, Pennsylvania. The camp was an outreach of First Presbyterian Church, Pittsburgh. The photo was in a pink paperback book called *How to Be Your Own Selfish Pig* by Susan Schaeffer Macaulay. Her name grabbed my attention, as by that time I was a burgeoning fan of her father, Francis A. Schaeffer. Written with total irony, much as Erasmus' *Praise of Folly*, Macaulay teased out a call for a new generation of Christians who would dare to act out their faith, not as disembodied missionaries, but as embodied ambassadors. She was calling upon earthlings like me to serve a world that God loved enough to visit personally. Of course, the principles impacted me as I headed back to the specific place called Bloomsburg University in northeastern Pennsylvania. I had met Becky there and we served as student leaders in Christian groups. "Bloom" was also the first place I felt connected to Christ as a living person, in my freshmen year. Between dorm life, retreats, and a continual round of shared meals, undergraduate life proved to be an ideal laboratory for living out an integrated life. And we had the added stress and benefit of figuring out what it means to be Christian on a diverse, secular, and spiritually apathetic campus.

I not only wanted to work out some of the principles I encountered in Susan's book, I also wanted to go to where they originated. Would I ever feel that lush grass on my bare feet and experience the life of the Manor House? The place I read about was L'Abri (meaning "the shelter," in French), a residential study center in Jane Austen country; a place where students and staff live, work, dine, play, and rest in community. I didn't make it to the English L'Abri when I was in college, but I kept reading Dr. Schaeffer's books. It would not be until January 1999 that seven Beckers would fly to London for a three-month stay there. Our brightly-colored and oh-so-American L.L.Bean duffle bags stood out in Heathrow Airport. We arrived bedraggled and jet lagged. I was to study my final Covenant Seminary class there via audio tape. We found ourselves crammed into a 700 square foot well house on the manor property in the dead of British winter. Meals and activities were shared with forty other students and staff in the damp and chilly brick mansion. Our daily routine was arduous with five kids in such a fishbowl. But it was rich. Then spring came, and we witnessed the magic of England up close.

It's ironic, isn't it, that most of us grow up in somewhat disintegrated settings: sitting in our screened-in porches, enjoying the view of our fenced-in backyards. Our tendency is to be isolated from neighbors, and yet we retain a longing for human proximity. It comes out on vacation. James Howard Kunstler opened my eyes to this when he suggested why we are attracted to certain holiday spots we might never choose to live in: a quaint New England seaside town, Disney World, or New York City, for example. These places share one thing: density and diversity, and a dose of the wild. The only time we experience this kind of human closeness, sadly, is when we have no other choice: college, prison, military, or the nursing home. Given the chance to fashion our ideal life setting, we imitate Thomas Jefferson. Apparently he disliked towns. He designed his Hermitage as a model of household *shalom:* living off the land, far away from others, out in the fresh, country air. Typical housing developments promise both distance from neighbors and nearness to services, yet they end up delivering neither well. Still, our impulse to pioneer our own plot of land and live quietly runs deep in our American psyche.

What can we do to engage our culture today in keeping with the physical settings we find ourselves in? It begins by simply taking that step back to notice where we are. While in my writing displacement in Florida, Chris Clark and his wife were happy to host me for five nights. During the day, I scribbled down random thoughts, and in the evenings I was part of their family. Chris was eager for me to meet his pastor and to discuss cultural engagement. I admit I felt a bit like the wrong guy for the task. Lakeland is radically unlike Lancaster City. It's flat, tropical, and thoroughly suburban except for a tiny town center. It's a fairly dense place, but I'm speaking now of the alligator population. The Clarks' church sits along Florida Avenue on the very edge of the large, incorporated city. Here I was, Northeastern City Guy, with all my thoughts about town living. What could I add to the discussion? I determined to listen and simply ask questions to discern the degree to which Chris and Lyle understood their exact place. Pastor Lyle is quite an apologist for his Lakeland. It's sunny often and halfway between Orlando and Tampa. He loves it there. But he also acknowledged that his people almost seem to like it too much. Families are in constant motion and partake in the luxuries of tropical life. Time together as a church family is a precious resource. Before I could ask him about being a bridge in this culture, his face lit up, and he began to speak about a citywide prayer journal one of his leaders has created. It was creating connections for people. His church is finding ways to not just understand their cultural setting, nor to throw their hands up in the air and give up. Instead, they are making the most of their situation, with all its beauty and complexity. They are beginning to love the ones they're with.

ENDNOTES

1. Ecclesiastes 3:11 (ESV).
2. Eric O Jacobsen, *Sidewalks in the Kingdom: New Urbanism and the Christian Faith* (Grand Rapids, MI: Brazos Press, 2003).
3. Eric O Jacobsen, *The Space Between: A Christian Engagement with the Built Environment* (Grand Rapids, MI: Baker Publishing Group, 2012).
4. Craig Bartholomew, *Where Mortals Dwell: A Christian View of Place for Today* (Grand Rapids, MI: Baker Publishing Group, 2011.
5. Augustine, and F. R. Montgomery Hitchcock. 1922. *St. Augustine's treatise on the City of God.* London: Society for Promoting Christian Knowledge.
6. Bruce Cockburn, "The Rose Above the Sky," *Humans* (True North, 1980).
7. Romans 16:20 (ESV).
8. 1 Corinthians 2:9 (ESV).

CREATIVITY

LIFE'S A PARTY

FUN IS CLOSELY RELATED TO JOY—
A SORT OF EMOTIONAL FROTH ARISING FROM THE
PLAY INSTINCT. IT IS VERY LITTLE USE TO US [DEMONS].
IT CAN SOMETIMES BE USED, OF COURSE, TO DIVERT
HUMANS FROM SOMETHING ELSE WHICH THE ENEMY
[GOD] WOULD LIKE THEM TO BE FEELING OR DOING:
BUT IN ITSELF IT HAS WHOLLY UNDESIRABLE
TENDENCIES; IT PROMOTES CHARITY, COURAGE,
CONTENTMENT, AND MANY OTHER EVILS.

—Screwtape, a senior tempter from
The Screwtape Letters by C.S. Lewis

It used to be that icebreakers were the brunt of jokes. Whether it's a youth gathering or adult garden party, we all know the awkwardness of Three Truths and a Lie, or Carry the Egg on the Spoon, or I Love You Baby Won't You Please Laugh (as you sit on a stranger's knee, attempting to make her laugh without laughing yourself). And yet, the leading late night talk host as I write is Jimmy Fallon. His stock-in-trade is the icebreaker. I can't be the only one who is pleasantly astonished. Not only because he's simply aping decades of zany games and stunts that had been going on in church basements for decades, but also because he's so incredibly popular. Celebrities of all kinds find themselves eagerly playing beer pong, competing in egg Russian roulette, or lip-synching to all manner of pop songs. Jimmy welcomes silliness and good clean fun in our pervasive culture of perversity. His monologues, too, packed as they are with shots at very important people, tend to be without guile and good-natured. Childlikeness reigns on *The Tonight Show*. I wouldn't call his nightcap a devotional, but it sure beats the local news and many other hosts who tend to traffic in cynicism.

When Jim Rayburn started Young Life as an outreach to un-churched kids, his motto was, "It's a sin to bore a kid." Today, Young Life camps offer top-notch accommodations in breathtaking environs. I've been to Lake Champion in New York, and I can assure you that the lodgings, the zip line, and the thirty-five-person hot tub are in no way boring. Imagine being a kid who is introduced, perhaps for the first time, to the person of Jesus in that context. No wonder many church leaders in American today can trace their spiritual inquisitiveness back to a Young Life experience in high school. Is it a sin to bore a kid? Most certainly. And if that's the case, and if Jesus Himself declared that only children can enter His Dad's kingdom, then it holds true that it's a sin to bore anyone. That is, He created a wild and wonderful world. He created image-bearers who are a world unto themselves. Not only is His creation marvelous, His ways with people east of Eden are no less amazing.

According to King David in Psalm 2, Yahweh sits on His throne and laughs in derision at all usurpers of His glory. The early converts to Christ quoted Psalm 2 when under persecution. God's laughter emboldened them to plead with God, "Consider now their threats, and enable your servants to speak with boldness!"[1] Though their situation was no laughing matter, these beleaguered believers found themselves caught up in God's victorious derision. I imagine a few of them actually laughing with joy. This is the kind of humor that peeps through the narrative of the book of Ruth. Naomi, after she loses her husband and two sons to famine, says, "Don't call me Naomi anymore. Call me Mara." She literally wants to be called "bitter" to reflect the bitter pill Yahweh, her God, shoved into her mouth. It's easy to read this very soberly and say, "Oh, she was so distraught that she sinned by getting angry and cynical." But the text doesn't read that way. Her exaggerated pity party just hangs there. But her honesty in the face of destitution is a hallmark of the Jewish sense of humor, which they learned from their God. Tevye in *Fiddler on the Roof* continually jostles with his God in a similar, laughable fashion. There's an old joke about the Jewish mother who loses her small son in the surf at the beach. The riptides take the boy out beyond reach, and he goes under. The mother pleads to God for his return. The kid bobs out of the water and washes up on the beach, alive. She takes one look at her beloved son, cocks her head to heaven, and reminds God with disappointment, "He had a hat!" It's as if God were a person and wanted to be related to on a personal level. It's as if His peoples' words were not an object of His derision. In fact, He bends His ear instead. Later, when Ruth finds "refuge under His wings," Mara heartily rejoices, and, we assume, goes back to embracing the name Naomi, which means "pleasantness." So, if you can't laugh at her exasperation and name-calling, you may be missing out on a bunch of other subtle laugh tracks in Scripture, not the least of which is Psalm 2. That our fallen experience is fallen is not funny. But since we're wired for laughter, sometimes it's the only way to get through life.

I've always been haunted by a single background vocal line in the song "She's Leaving Home" by Lennon and McCartney. The ballad tells of a young girl leaving a note and taking up a new, wild life with "a man from the motor trade." The parents are portrayed as heartbroken for their little girl who's "leaving home after living alone for so many years." The mantra "she's leaving home" in the background changes to "she's having fun," and the parental voices answer, "Fun is the one thing that money can't buy." It's a bit corny, but the notion of a child feeling trapped by adults who take themselves too seriously is one we can all relate to at some level. For my part, I didn't really relate to this kind of suppression until I got into Christianity. My personality definitely lends itself to being the life of the party, it's true. And I have the knee pain to prove it after each coveted dance party in which I take part. I've found, then, in Christianity a sort of somberness related to engaging with our culture. For, after all, the apologetic aspect of faith (its defense in a watching world) is a task worthy of deep contemplation, careful analysis, and intelligent rhetoric. Actually, though, the toolbox we've been given for proclaiming Christ to the world is a lot more brilliantly-faceted than that. Some of our tools are wonder, surprise, hyperbole, subversion, mystery, humor, and (can I say it?) absurdity. There's also a huge difference between taking our Lord seriously and taking ourselves seriously. This is not to say our message is absurd; nothing could be further from the truth. The only real absurdity, according to Scripture, is unbelief. But belief doesn't, *ipso facto,* require complete sobriety an all occasions.

I wonder if Christians might be more effective in our day with a dose of serious lightheartedness about our place in the world. It is refreshing when a Christian in a popular art form is portrayed as an everyday earthling and not as a pearly white saint, abusive demagogue, or anal-retentive hypocrite. In a meet-and-greet I attended featuring actor Doug Jones, he shared a story of helping to rewrite a screenplay. He was to portray a psychopath living on the top floor of an apartment building, one he was systematically destroying.

The writer had called for the bad guy's apartment to be lined with Bible verse cutouts. Doug, being a Christian, gently suggested, "Look, isn't this a bit cliché? Do you really need to portray this psycho as a loose cannon Christian? Can you think of something more creative?" The writer agreed and turned Doug's character into some other kind of weirdo. I think Doug's approach gives us a double example: first, he shows how to effect change in our sphere of influence by enabling our neighbors to take a step back from their utterly lock-tight, serious (and often misguided) assumptions about Christianity. And second, he demonstrates it in a way that is respectful, honest, and lighthearted.

I spoke for a youth leadership camp a few years back and got some significant pushback. Not from the staff, but from an unlikely place: the students. My theme was *Wired for Glory*. But it was my opening talk that put up a roadblock for a vocal minority of kids. That talk was called *Wired to Party*. I could see the youth leaders "uh-huh-ing" me every step of the way as I walked the students through a biblical theology of joy, celebration, and, yes, partying. I went from Sabbath feasts (they're not *fasts!*) to the seventy-year exile (brought on by Israel's refusal to keep Sabbath) to the wedding at Cana (where Jesus made the Best Wine Ever) to Lord's Day worship to the marriage supper of the Lamb. My point? God wants His people to party, in Him, for their good, for the world. I assumed the kids would appreciate it. Most did, but some were offended. They just couldn't get past the word "party." I suppose the opening slide of a bunch of rowdy kids at a rave didn't help either. But my point was that the world has a broken view of partying, a pathetically flat one, actually. We, as children of God, ought to throw the most joyful, fully human parties. Still, they couldn't get around that term. I was forced to ask why.

Maybe we've shown by example that emotions are dangerous, that celebrating at its core is tainted, and that true spirituality is at best an intellectual assent to doctrine (Gnosticism) and at worst an unquestioned acceptance of the culture of restraint (Stoicism). After my second talk, called *Wired for Friending*, the staff informed me of the the disengagement of the kids who were blindsided by my first talk. So, before my third talk, *Wired for Winning*, an exposé of the roots of ambition, I opened the group up for questions. I also made it clear that as a father, pastor, and speaker, the last thing I wanted to do was miscommunicate or, worse yet, do anything short of putting them in mind of our Lord Jesus. Thankfully, the staff had done a fantastic job of hearing the troubled kids out and reengaging them by helping them appreciate my rhetoric. They insisted, mercifully, that I was *not* a heretic. I was given the mornings to delve into something practical, something about engaging culture. So I created a competition for "The Funnest Event Ever." Pulling together six or so students from different churches, my goal was that they would build new friendships, spur creativity, and have a fun time working out how they might use fun apologetically in their own towns. The kids understood the experiment and had a great time. I was really impressed by their creativity once they were freed up to dream up a fun activity. I posed as a celebrity judge of their ideas as they pitched each one to me. Then I put the voting to "America," and the entire camp picked the winning event: a camp-wide, Olympics-style race that involved photos with watermelons, tests of skill, and a subsequent watermelon feast. By that time everyone was having a party, as far as I could tell. But I still wonder: why is our practice of Christianity so often lifeless? I believe it's because, in the end, we are not wise.

The book of Ecclesiastes is well known for its assertion, "vanities of vanities!" It's the book in the Bible that thoughtful Christians often prescribe to their friends who are either depressed or into philosophy. Not a bad idea, because it does affirm in no uncertain terms that life on this earth is random, monotonous, and ultimately vain: we die and lose everything. However, on closer examination you'll find that vanity, what the apostle Paul calls the groaning of creation in Romans 8, is not the chorus at all. Many readers find the key at the conclusion of the book, but that's a bit of a smokescreen: "Fear God and obey His commands. That is the end of the matter."[2] Well, that's all nice and tidy, but what does it look like to fear God? The writer of Ecclesiastes, known as The Preacher is a stand-in for King Solomon, the most celebrated and richest of all the kings of Israel. He's seen it all and bought the T-shirt factory. Since this is part of the wisdom literature of the Old Testament, one must ask, what is wisdom, then? It's in the chorus that appears no less than nine times in slightly different ways: "I perceived that there is nothing better for them than to be joyful and to do good as long as they live; also that everyone should eat and drink and take pleasure in all his toil—this is God's gift to man."[3]

The Preacher says there is joy to be found in this vain life no matter where it bends.[4] Throughout the Scripture, God invites His people to rejoice in the earthly existence He's given them. Nothing lasts forever. Laughter is achievable. Joy is possible. If we "fight for the right to party" in the most holy sense possible, our apologetic for the reality of Christ in us will be self-evident. And we will be doing what He's commanded us to do.

Laughing in the midst of our pained existence in solidarity with all people is a bridge to our friends—a bridge we need not be ashamed to be seen on. There's no need to start a Christian comedy tour as if laughter were only a means to an end. Our joy in the Spirit is a not an instrument nor is it an end in itself. It is our inheritance. It is, in fact, a down payment of joy everlasting.

One of our best friends and a devoted partner in The Row House is Kimberly. At a time when we hosted concerts, she invited a Chinese student she was hosting to our blues show at the Elks Lodge.[5] It featured legendary blues guitarist and vocalist Glenn Kaiser from Chicago. I connected Glenn to a bass player and an outstanding drummer. My daughter spearheaded a silent auction of LP's, a pink girls' bike, and some original art. We encouraged people to come in "vintage formal wear" (whatever that is). A group of blues dancers showed up, and as they danced on the sides, a freestyle dance party erupted in the back. The evening was supplemented with a cash bar, LP vinyl lounge, and a contest for the best dressed. In a subtle yet profound way, we achieved a Christ-centered event that was a blast. Apparently confused, Kimberly's student turned to her and said, "These are Christians?" She modestly affirmed that, yes, most of the people were. What made this event a triumph was the hilarity, the joy, and the sweet release of dancing the blues. If that girl only remembers that taste of joy, then it's not a large step for her to investigate the life of Jesus as someone worth getting to know.

Not all of our events are that raucous. At the hub of our events are the Forums. We make them a party in a few ways: first, as host, I put people at ease. I don't have to work at that part. I enjoy peppering the evening with my ironies and lightheartedness. Some of our topics are very serious indeed: the developing world, media binge-watching, and mental health. Others lend themselves to lighter moments: millennials, parenting, and mythology. In addition, I try to pair the food offerings with the topic. Our goal is to be approachable and permeable for folks who are less versed in Christianity, but we also want Christian people to have a great time. I try to demonstrate that laughter is not an instrument, nor is it our end; it's a taste of something. It's worth indulging in whenever possible.

I've heard that the great comedian Danny Kaye was very effective on tours of developing countries. The language barrier is always a problem when a white person lands in, say, a village in Nigeria. For one thing, Danny Kaye sported bright red hair. Automatically, he became an attraction. But what was he to do once the nationals noticed his tall, pale body with blazing hair?

He simply smiled and went about his routine of physical comedy, delighting kids, and spellbinding the adults. At the moment we feel we have nothing to give our culture, perhaps we need to give ourselves the gift of laughter. Maybe that's what Naomi unwittingly gave to her daughter-in-law Ruth through her extravagant grievance against God. Ruth clung to Naomi, bitter Naomi. Perhaps Naomi had a twinkle in her eye even as she lamented the death of her life as she knew it. Perhaps Ruth would rather follow Naomi's gracious God than the blood-hungry deities of her pagan upbringing. Perhaps she was drawn to God's party through the arguably laughable testimony of Naomi. All we know is that it worked. Ruth got herself a husband after the famine and became the grandmother of Kind David, the very poet who wrote Psalm 2. Now, that's funny.

In your context, there's bound to be someone who is a walking flower shop, someone who enjoys acknowledging special occasions. For me, it's Ned and Leslie Bustard. They would celebrate the anniversary of their car purchase if they could afford to. Seriously, with them I have enjoyed celebrating their children's' baptisms, our friends' landmark birthdays, or church calendar days that often go unnoticed (the Feasts of Saint Patrick, Saint Brendan, and Saint C.S. Lewis are among their favorites—please don't pop their bubble and tell them Lewis isn't a recognized saint). If you can find such a person in your group, you may want to promote them by giving them a title like "Offical Party Thrower." Let's throw a party for the party throwers among us! Don't offer to pay them. These professional celebrants will commemorate joyous occasions because it's part of their DNA. But lean on them. I do. I need a flower shop to remind me of important days, and that's what I have in the Bustards.

Anything a church or group of Christians can do that is fun, I'm all for it. Whatever is already planned to bring people together can be exploited to leverage more laughing and celebrating: picnics, coffee hours, retreats, even worship services. On the latter, I don't recommend drawing attention away from the "divine hour" of meeting with God, but there are appropriate ways to express joy and humor. My preference for worship services, based on this notion of being fully human, is a combination of high liturgy and casualness. Some church cultures are much more comfortable with bumps in the service, touch, and joking around. Others need to lighten up a bit.

Meanwhile, American culture is on a high with promoting fun, even at an outrageous cost. For instance, what city needs a 5K race where people run through clouds of sticky, brightly-colored dust? On the other hand, what city can do without one? Be that as it may, any number of activities in our community are built-in opportunities to drive the party bus. In Lancaster, the Long's Park Amphitheater organization sponsors free lawn concerts on Sunday evening. Thousands of people attend to hear a range of musical expressions. Picnics and dogs are encouraged. Often, we sit with a gaggle of church folk at these community-building events. As small group leaders, we encourage these concerts as a social platform for catching up and simply being present in the broader community. But the bottom line is, they are fun. And fun is good because God wired us to party! Not only that, but . . . err, excuse me, I'll be right back—my Frisbee is calling.

ENDNOTES

1. Acts 4:29 (ESV).
2. Ecclesiastes 12:13, 14 (author's paraphrase).
3. Ecclesiastes 3:12,13 (ESV).
4. Ecclesiastes 9:9 (ESV): "Enjoy life with your wife, whom you love, all the days of this meaning-less life that God has given you under the sun—all your meaningless days. For this is your lot in life and in your toilsome labor under the sun."
5. Originally begun as the Lancaster Buffalo Club in 1889 by a group of twenty-four men who wished to exchange their horns for antlers.

BECOME A CHILD AGAIN

THE STUMBLER DOESN'T AIM FOR JOY.
JOY IS A BYPRODUCT EXPERIENCED BY PEOPLE
WHO ARE AIMING FOR SOMETHING ELSE.
BUT IT COMES.

—David Brooks, *The Road to Character*

My Dad put a pool table in our unfinished basement. To dress the place up, I suppose, he hung signs typically found in dive bars. Beer names like Carlburg, Schlitz, and Pabst were as familiar to me as Bible book titles to church kids. Backlit, plastic, and bold, one sign remains indelibly etched in my memory. It pictured a young woman riding on the shoulders of her man while he casually surfs into shore. As an eight-year-old boy, I would flick the chrome toggle switch at its rear. The image of the beach-bodied beauties simply leapt to life. Enraptured, I dug my thumbnail into its soft plastic screen, creating a tiny white bruise, so lustful was I to enter its shimmering world. Despite several searches on the Internet, I've yet to uncover any trace of the sign. In mourning for that flicker of ineffable joy, I could only write a poem. If you can bear with my amateur pen, here are a few stanzas:

A cobalt, backlit, luminescent breaker
White-capped, floats the hang-tenners
like a maître d's graceful arc

A Blue so sublime, so alive, deep
in my memory as vivid
as my Dad's Aqua Velva aftershave

Hung by a common nail on a block wall
Lewis surprised by joy, Pascal on fire
Blue I've longed to smell again just once

For C.S. Lewis, his first experience of such joy came while gazing on a pie plate on which his brother had constructed a childlike diorama. Something ineffable came over him too, and when I read his words in early adulthood in *Surprised by Joy*, I found myself in the basement again. What happened to that sign? Why do I so rarely experience transcendent joy? As we emerge from childhood, the wonder of creation, imagination, and play give way to self-consciousness. I recall two moments when I began *thinking* about my thinking. On our hunting farm in Muncy, Pennsylvania, I spent a night in a dank mobile home with my Dad, brothers, and some hunting buddies. In the night, the trailer rattled, and we started at what sounded like a sonic boom. The next morning, as we were winding our way into the woods under the cover of darkness, we came upon the source of the sound. A lightning bolt had split a mammoth pine down the middle, destroying fully half of its canopy. Prior to that evening, I would ride my three-wheeler into the woods, bend under its low-hanging branches, and gaze up into its cathedral of branches. A perfect circle. The morning after it was felled, I pulled warm, aromatic shards of white pine from its shattered torso. I was rattled by the revelation of the heretofore unseen, utterly pure pulp at the core of its being. "Am I seen? Who sees me in the lonely forest? Am I alone?" The second reckoning of my existence happened on the steps of Bucknell University in 1979. I was attending a six-week arts immersion school. I was sixteen. I closed my eyes on that humid summer night and listened to the world around me for the first time as a subject. Tires on pavement, robins chirping, huddles of students chatting in the distance across the street. I knew then I was alive. I existed . . . and I was in fact alone, but I also felt important.

And so I travelled, unknowingly, from blissful ignorance to the inhibition of self-knowledge, skepticism, and shame. The next step for all of us, it seems to me, is anxiety. I'm a slow bloomer in general. Acute anxiety mercifully did not overtake me until I was in my forties. But like many of my late Baby Boomer brethren, I became motivated toward adulthood responsibility by an imagination of what could go wrong. That is, working to support my family became my preoccupation. My work may have been religious in nature, but I tried to avoid spiritualizing it. I just worked hard, but I did maintain a strain of childlike joy. My sense of curiosity, humor, and fitness kept me from being consumed by responsibility. Plus, having kids in sweet succession sent me back to the nursery, literally. I did not grow up with children's books as Becky had, and I thoroughly enjoyed entering all the great stories with my girls. I discovered *Little House on the Prairie, Charlotte's Web,* and Richard Scarry. Staying in touch with childhood makes me particularly moved by adolescents who go quickly from wonder to self-consciousness to anxiety. Sometimes a song will stop me in my tracks. If I'm in my car, I sit for one of those driveway moments. If I'm on my bicycle, I pull over. Usually, my eyes well up with grief or joy. I must be quite a sight. Such an epiphany hit me when I heard "Stressed Out" by Twenty One Pilots for the first time.

> Wish we could turn back time, to the good ol' days,
> When our momma sang us to sleep but now we're stressed out.
> Used to play pretend, used to play pretend, bunny
> We used to play pretend, wake up, you need the money
> We used to play pretend, give each other different names,
> We would build a rocket ship and then we'd fly it far away,
> Used to dream of outer space but now they're laughing at our face,
> Saying, "Wake up, you need to make money."[1]

It seems each generation finds a way to express the grief of childhood lost. In 1980, the year I graduated high school, Pink Floyd's "Comfortably Numb" put it this way:

> When I was a child I caught a fleeting
>   glimpse out of the corner of my eye.
> I turned to look but it was gone.
> I cannot put my finger on it now.
> The child is grown.
> The dream is gone.
> I have become comfortably numb.[2]

The good news of Christ is that you can become a child again. It's simple. Stand outside on a clear night, away from the light pollution of street lamps. Look up. I once asked twenty college students to do this with me, smack dab in the middle of a talk I was giving them on Psalm 8. We stood in the gravel parking lot in Millersville University, awkwardly shifting stones on sneakers. "Now look up," I prodded them. I picture King David doing this. With all his power, responsibilities, and burdens as Israel's monarch, I see him musing under the stars, strumming his six-string. And this is a paraphrase of the lyric he wrote:

> What is man that you are mindful of him,
>   the son of man that you take note of him?
> You made him a little lower the angels
>   and crowned him with glory and honor.
> O Lord, our Lord, how majestic is your name in all the earth!
> From the lips of small children
>   you have ordained praise to silence the foe and the avenger.

There is a common understanding in our science-soaked worldview that looking up at the stars puts us in our place. Such contemplation only reinforces how insignificant and small we are. But this was not David's assessment. Quite the opposite, actually. The universe did in fact put him in his place. And that place is that God is mindful of him, creating in him praise and appreciation for his own worth. The writer of the New Testament letter to the Hebrews picks up on David's verse and applies it to Jesus. Christ was no angel. He was better than that; He was human, crowned with glory and honor. In Him, Christians can and should look up and become children again, because that is what they are. And this thought should not put us in a place of puniness but of beloved grandeur. Little children know this intuitively. Here's my Dad. Here's my Mom. I will look up to them. I know nothing else, nothing better. This was the purpose of Matthew Dickerson's first visit to The Row House: to spur a little childlikeness.

Matthew is a true renaissance man: Professor of Computer Science at Middlebury College in Vermont; author of books on fly fishing, mythology, and music; musician; father; husband; global lecturer. He is smart and absolutely approachable. I invited him to speak directly about wonder in the most child-like and wonderful venue we've ever worked with: The Rabbit & Dragonfly Cafe. This place is themed around the British writers known as the Inklings, such as J.R.R. Tolkien, Dorothy Sayers, Charles Williams, and C.S. Lewis. The owners are some of the warmest and most whimsical characters in Lancaster. It's a privilege to partner with such dear friends. Dr. Dickerson enhanced their cave-like vibe with an outstanding lecture on the roots of Tolkien's wonder in the grand story of Beowulf and Nordic myth. He tied the quest of the Hobbits to the suffering and courage that will ultimately defeat evil. He said a lot more, and folks couldn't get enough of his brain in the Q&A time. What I appreciate even more than Matthew's scholarship and intelligence is his vital childlikeness. He's a joyful soul who loves fly fishing and performing music. Perhaps he is a Renaissance Kid?

If you're paying attention, you might wonder why I would ask Matthew to talk directly about the topic. Isn't analyzing something so sublime the antithesis of simply experiencing it firsthand? Yes, it can happen, and I've seen this over-explanation of beauty gut the very medium of its power. For instance, a preacher droning on about the beauties of Hebrew poetry. I want to stand up and implore him, "Please stop talking! Can we just recite the Psalm together? Or could you write a tune and sing the words?" I took the risk of sidestepping the inherent power of myth through a lecture, knowing that somehow Matthew would not only deliver didactic points of interest, but he would also spin the talk into something magical. He did. And, as I said, the venue itself spoke to our senses in memorable ways.

Childlike wonder and the pursuit of joy are elusive. Sometimes a glimpse is all you need to keep believing in their existence. David Brooks calls these moments "limerence."[3] It's when everything seems to cohere or when we experience human intimacy. It is a taste of what God has planed for those who love Him. When you stop pursuing limerence, that might mean you've grown up, in the wrong way. It might mean that you're using your imagination to picture the worst. That's anxiety taking over. And anxiety is a very grown-up malady.

I'm not a worrisome person, nor do I battle chronic anxiety or sudden panic, as some of my dear friends do. Most days, I battle anxiety in some form, though. A thought of shame, destitution, or misgiving lights up in my synapses. I often wonder, what is the source of my anxiety? Why is it that one moment I feel a pit in my stomach, then the next moment the pit is replaced with a sense of giddy expectancy? More to the point, why am I *not* more anxiety-ridden than I am? There are many realities I could be anxious about: the possibility of losing my functions, the plight of Syrian refugees, or my fear of needles. Ninety-eight percent of the time, when I'm feeling healthy or not particularly tired, I just live. I'm like a little kid, splitting lanes downtown on my bike, making revving noises in my throat. So, why shouldn't any of us be in a constant state of fear? Recently I sat in a dentist's chair for nearly an hour with my mouth propped open while a specialist reamed out my canals. I thought, "Man, this would suck if I had anxiety about dentistry." It made me grateful. I fly in airplanes in a heartbeat, but I cannot sleep in a car. Why? It makes me anxious. I imagine the worst. What I've learned is this: the source of my anxiety is not insufficient funds, debt, the IRS, relational disappointments, toilsome work, uncertain funding, or the expectations of others. The source of my anxiety is my imagination. The world rotates fine without me. God still sits on His throne caring for creation without me. Life goes on, and my fears amount to nothing.

The Row House, in its early years, kept me perennially anxious about money. I had experienced a tough ten years of uncertainty as a campus minister and schoolteacher. Though Becky had started a neighborhood school, our combined incomes were never near a living wage. Keeping credit at bay and humbling ourselves before our concerned parents wore on us. Just about the time we were stabilizing our paltry nonprofit start-up salaries, the IRS came knocking. They said I owed $6,500 from a three years past botched return. I had to laugh. I hired a lawyer and got the bill down to about half that much. I had to constantly remind myself that I had advantages as a middle-class white person that many people in my own city never had. At the heart, I've learned I'm mostly anxious about failing. I hear the Anxious Adult voice saying I could've done more for my kids. Then my Emerging Child answers back: *It's not my job to provide for my family. It's God's job to do it through me. I gave my kids presence, wisdom and as much provision as I could muster considering my calling in life. Take a hike, Anxiety!*

What does all this have to do with engaging culture? Everything. If our natural progression is from faith to doubt to fear, the way back to being God's child in this world is to backtrack. We need to look our adult anxiety straight in the eye, address our doubts, and get back to childlike wonder. Our culture already values escape. NASCAR weekends, blockbuster films, and the occasional carnival attractions remind me that deep down, we seek joy. Our thirst is never quite slaked, of course, but the quest is human and valuable. There are several unique ways Christians can get on this highway back to joy. If we go that route, instead of the route of seriousness often associated with religious life, we might recover ourselves and engage our neighbors at the same time. My Border-Retriever mix named Rue gets anxious, but she doesn't battle anxiety. She just reacts to uncomfortable or threatening situations. Humans do this too, thanks to adrenaline. Acute anxiety is to be expected. It's a defense system. But after the adrenaline dissipates and the crisis is over, what's left? We have God-implanted imagination. If only we'd reengage our imaginations toward childlike wonder in those times when we are at leisure to exercise it. Too often, we squash our imagination through binge-watching when we could take up meditating, sketching, or laughing with children. I want The Row House to be a playground for imagination to move people back from the cliff of anxiety into healthy self-reflection, ultimately leading to renewed hope.

I've always enjoyed the visual arts. In the very basement where I stood gazing into the ocean blue in a barroom sign, I built a miniature town. To qualify for the Governors's School for the Arts, I created a Super 8 short film in which my HO scale town came to life. It got me in the summer program, but no George Lucas was I. To this day I see life compositionally. I still shoot 35mm film and dabble in absurd short documentaries for friends. Some people think I run an strange snow globe business from my basement, but I can't really comment on that. I contribute concepts to all of our Row House designs. I insist on keeping my life and my life's work whimsical. Somehow, it comes naturally to me, but there have been moments I've forgotten who I am. Those moments, now that I've started The Row House, are lessening daily. If asked if I'm an artist, I happily say, "Well, no, I'm not a working artist. But I do collect artists." Most of my friends are either generating income from creative endeavors, or they are artful in their way of life. If I enjoy showcasing artists it's because I believe they are the sanest people of all. Even the really eccentric ones. I recently spoke with a geeky college girl who was well-versed in the mythological universe called Marvel Comics. I thought, this kid has promise. Stan Lee was also once a wide-eyed, dreamy, sketchbook-toting nerd, spinning characters and story lines about so-called super heroes. A select few followers found solace and even a fair amount of meaning in his characters. Now, Mr. Lee is himself a super hero. Who would've ever guessed his universe would give rise to the biggest film movement in cinematic history? This young girl who knows precisely how The Guardians of the Galaxy are related to The Fantastic Four is no head-in-the-clouds escapist. She knows what matters most: allowing her imagination to remind her that she is in fact, a super hero, mightily treasured by a heavenly father who made her just the way He wanted her. I'm beginning to understand my status, as well. My art is curation. I show off other people. To curate, in its original sense, is to *cure* at a deep spiritual level.

All of us need to know where we stand. Who are we? What are we worth? In the Gospel according to Luke, Jesus conducts a job review with His disciples. It's vital to understand that they already got the job. He sent seventy-two of His closest friends out with the commission to heal the sick, cast out demons, and preach His Father's good news. They come back to Him after a very successful trip and Jesus basically says, "Don't throw a party yet." He concedes that, yes, lots of miracles happened and that it was amazing. But then He says, "Rejoice in this: that your names are written in heaven." Is He a killjoy? Names written in heaven: what's that? In Exodus, chapter 37 we see God's instructions to Moses for how the Jews were to worship in their new tabernacle. As part of that the High Priest was to be clothed in a symbolically pregnant way. He was to carry with him on his shoulders the names of the twelve tribes of Israel, engraved on two precious stones. And tied to those shoulder pads, he wore a covering on his chest called an *ephod,* bearing twelve more precious stones, each inscribed with a tribal name. As the priest visited with God in the Holy of Holies, he would be bearing, symbolically, the sons of Israel into God's presence, near to his heart. Back to Jesus' friends. Whether things go well again, or they go south (and they were sure to go south; all the twelve disciples but one were brutalized for their association with Jesus), it shouldn't matter. Simply by calling the seventy-two into His mission of joy, He's saying, "Your greatest reward is that God Himself treasures you; you are held fast to His heart." It follows that Christians are hidden with Christ in God, as Paul says it. Being treasured by God the Father is your greatest treasure. This is a cause for rejoicing. To have your name written in heaven might look like this picture from the second chapter of John's Revelation, the seventeenth verse: "He who has an ear, let him hear what the Spirit says to the churches. To the one who conquers I will give some of the hidden manna, and I will give him a white stone, with a new name written on the stone that no one knows except the one who receives it."

Nobody knows what this renaming ceremony will look like, but it's worth imagining. Maybe God's loved ones will be given a stone with a name only God knows. I like to think that about myself, especially on the days when I feel like my name is mud. Perhaps the secret name between me and Jesus is *Augustine Bono Lionhearted Thomas Dartt Becker Faithful to the End, Friend to Many.* That's a fine one, but I'm sure that the real one is even better. Whatever name you could wish God your Father would call you, His name for you is greater than you can imagine. He knows who you are, and when you meet Him face to face and He uses that name, you won't be a bit surprised by joy.

If anyone is convinced his name is written in heaven, it's Bob Goff. He's achieved a lot as an attorney, speaker, and leader. He lives on the coast in San Diego. He has it all. But he wears no golden handcuffs. He tossed them off long ago. Among other accolades, he serves as Honorary Consul for the Republic of Uganda to the United States. In his book, *Love Does,* Bob describes the

Ugandans' first visit to his office. They were quite surprised and delighted, I'm sure, to find he often meets his high-powered clients on Tom Sawyer Island. At Disneyland. Meeting dignitaries in such a childlike setting works to his advantage, as it taps into a deep-seated wonder at the heart of even the most serious, jaded, and cynical adults he encounters. Plus, it's just cool.

Jesus wouldn't have said, "Rejoice that your names are written in heaven" if it weren't true or it weren't possible. Believe the Good News: it's true. Live the Good News: you can find your way to joy again. You can become a child again. You can, literally, *re-joice*.

Who can forget Gene Wilder's portrayal of Willie Wonka? After nearly crushing young Charlie's spirits, Mr. Wonka gently arrests the young boy's hand, turns, and says, "Charlie, dear child, you've won! I had to test you, Charlie. I had to find a sweet, innocent child. Because a grown-up would've spoiled everything." In the Wonkavator Charlie asks about the lifetime supply of chocolate. And here's where I conflate Wonka's words with Jesus': "The chocolate, yes, Charlie. Yes, of course, you're getting all that. But don't rejoice in that. Rejoice in this: I'm giving you the whole factory, Charlie. It's yours." Our commission by Jesus to engage culture isn't a test to see if we're worthy of the job. We're already employed. He's called a ragtag gaggle of kids into His unassailable mission of joy. Let us engage our current culture with ancient faith from a wellspring of joy. Let us be spellbound by God's spell. Let us be ravished by the spectacle of the splicing of heaven and earth, all to His glory.

ONE MORE THING

From that sublime thought, I must come in for a landing.

One of the toughest parts of writing this book was coming up with a title. I knew I wanted to include the concept of bridge-building I had learned through my years of life on campus, in settings like L'Abri Fellowship, and sitting under Jerram Barrs and the faculty at Covenant Theological Seminary. But this book has been less about building a bridge and more about getting on the bridge God has already made. What's it look like to be out on the human bridge?

The word "posture" kept coming back to me. And then Grandma Becker's face appeared like a specter. Put more accurately, her back-hander emerged from my past as she swatted me across the shoulder and said, "Stop your slouching!" Florence Dartt Becker was rough on us teenage boys. She only had to slap me once. I always knew how to carry myself in her presence!

Good Posture. That was the perfect title for this book. When I passed the idea on to the creative director of Square Halo Books, I got sent back to me the quirky cover design that currently wraps this book. You surely noticed the brave, mustachioed daredevil pictured on the front. He was a Frenchman who went by the name Monsieur Charles Blondin. Born in 1825, by the time he gave his final performance in 1896 he had crossed Niagara Falls three hundred times on a tightrope. Each successive crossing become more splendid. His antics included walking backwards, crossing blindfolded, and stopping to cook an omelette and lower it to the *Maid of the Mist* boat hundreds of feet below him.

Now, you'd think we picked Chuck for his eloquent balance. After all, Christians should be balanced in the way they approach the world around them. Engaged, but not too entrapped. Holy, but not overly righteous, and so on. But I actually prefer the concept of posture over balance. Speaking of the Christian life in terms of balance can lead to complacency in the name of carefulness, and ambivalence in times of emergency. Notwithstanding all its wonderful possibilities—such as moderation, male/female complementarity, and the daily rhythm of day and night—balance is not the best metaphor for engaging our world.

Just look at Jesus' life on earth, and you'll see it was nothing short of spurts of intensity mixed with stretches of mundanity. He laughed with children and stood up to bullies. His sermons were peppered with miracles, and His shining moment, according to Him, was His tortured death on a Roman cross. Hardly a balanced human life.

But His posture was rooted in love for His Father. What flowed out from that was a stance of holiness that His people to this day are enjoined to maintain. As the Apostle puts it, our essential posture in spiritual warfare is simply to stand in Christ (Ephesians 6:11).

In the end, Mr. Blondin's career was rooted in his good posture, which gave rise to the balance he desperately needed inch by inch.

Before heading back over Niagara Falls to America from Canada, he put his own manager on his back and said, "Look up, Harry . . . you are no longer Colcord, you are Blondin. Until I clear this place, be a part of me, mind, body, and soul. If I sway, sway with me. Do not attempt to do any balancing yourself. If you do we will both go to our death."[5]

If we stand, let us stand confidently in Christ and engage our culture for His glory.

> So if I stand let me stand on the promise
> That you will pull me through
> And if I can't let me fall on the grace
> That first brought me to You
> —Rich Mullins, "If I Stand," *Winds of Heaven, Stuff of Earth*

I hope my words and my story have encouraged you no matter where you are in this spectacle called God's Kingdom. Maybe you're skeptical about its very existence—*take a second look.* Maybe you feel you have little to offer—*stop your slouching.* Maybe you're full of yourself—*become a child again.*

ENDNOTES

1. Tyler Joseph, "Stressed Out," Blurryface (*Fueled by Ramen,* 2015).
2. David Gilmour and Roger Waters, "Comfortably Numb," *The Wall* (New York City: Columbia Records, 1979).
3. David Brooks, *The Social Animal: The Hidden Sources of Love, Character, and Achievement* (New York: Random House, 2011).
4. 1 Corinthians 2:9 (ESV).
5. Karen Abbott, "The Daredevil of Niagara Falls," Smithsonian.com, October 18, 2011, https://www.smithsonianmag.com/history/the-daredevil-of-niagara-falls-110492884/.

DISCUSSION QUESTIONS

BRIDGEKEEPER: STOP! HE WHO WOULD CROSS THE
BRIDGE OF DEATH MUST ANSWER ME THESE
QUESTIONS THREE, ERE THE OTHER SIDE
HE SEE. SIR LANCELOT: ASK ME YOUR QUESTIONS,
BRIDGEKEEPER. I AM NOT AFRAID. BRIDGEKEEPER:
WHAT . . . IS YOUR NAME? SIR LANCELOT: SIR
LANCELOT OF CAMELOT. BRIDGEKEEPER: WHAT . . .
IS YOUR QUEST? SIR LANCELOT: TO SEEK THE HOLY
GRAIL. BRIDGEKEEPER: WHAT . . . IS YOUR FAVORITE
COLOR? SIR LANCELOT: BLUE. BRIDGEKEEPER: RIGHT,
OFF YOU GO.

—Scene 22, *Monty Python and the Holy Grail*

Though the following questions will be useful for individual reflection, I've written them to be used in small groups. You will notice a progression based loosely on The Row House's purpose of "engaging current culture with ancient faith." The beginning questions relate to fixed realities from the past, the middle ones relate to your current experience, and the latter ones point you to the future. The books listed serve a dual purpose: they showcase some of the sources for my thinking over the years, and they provide a rich resource for your group discussions and further reflection.

WHAT I DO

1. List some of the ways the people of Israel "remembered" the works of God in their history.
2. What role does memory and reenactment play in your experience of Christianity, past or present?
3. Describe a "phoenix" moment in your life when everything you cared about seemed to be burned to the ground. How did it change you? What did you learn? How do you remember (or forget) it?
4. Grab a pencil. In three paragraphs, describe in detail three of your proudest achievements from three general epochs of your life (e.g., grammar school, teen years, college, young adult, etc.). They need not be accomplishments in the eyes of others; simply things you enjoyed doing and took pride in. Focus on how you did them. Then, with a close friend or small group, discuss:
   • To what extent are we using the abilities we enjoy using most?
   • Why would we hold back from using our motivated abilities?
   • How can we better lean into our strengths?
   • What new direction, work, or adventure is stirring in us?

RECOMMENDED READING

Stephen A. Cooper, *Augustine for Armchair Theologians* (Louisville/London: Westminster John Knox Press, 2002).
Jonathan Wilson-Hartgrove, *The Wisdom of Stability: Rooting Faith in a Mobile Culture* (Brewster, MA: Paraclete Press, 2010).
Andy Crouch, *Culture Making: Recovering Our Creative Calling* (Downers Grove, IL: InterVarsity Press, 2008).

QUICK TO LISTEN

1. Some in the Hebrew tradition believe the first commandment to the Israelites was, "Listen up!" Consider the prologue to the Ten Commandments: "Hear, O Israel: The Lord our God, the Lord is one.[a] 5 You shall love the Lord your God with all your heart and with all your soul and with all your might" (Deuteronomy 6:4–5).
   - Have you experienced firsthand, or can you imagine, a nonreading culture? Describe their experience with the task of listening.
   - Is our current interest in listening to podcasts a sign of human flourishing or human degradation (i.e., away from visual literacy)?
2. Observe your surrounding culture's practice of listening.
   - What is your region, town, or neighborhood known for in terms of interpersonal communication? Are they brash? Reserved? Easily offended? Openhearted?
   - How does your "tribe" (closest peer group) communicate?
   - Is there a history of learning and listening in your household or church?
   - Where is listening most needed in your neck of the woods?
3. Conduct a conversational role play. With an unsuspecting friend or in groups of two within your group, carry on a five-minute chat with someone while ruthlessly abiding by these rules: *Make no "bald" statements about anything (don't say anything uncalled-for by your partner). Instead, ask questions to keep the conversation going, and answer your partner's questions or repeat their statements in a show of listening.* Just be brief. Evaluate the conversation by taking a few notes:
   - Did my friend seem to notice my strategy?
   - What was difficult for me?
   - How did this exercise pave the way for understanding on either side?
   - Was it awkward?
   - What feelings did I have at the conclusion? Were they different from how I usually exit a conversation?

4. Make a list of the types of cultural input you need to increase. For instance:
   - If you only read fiction, introduce other genres to expand your understanding of people and the world: poetry, history, general non-fiction, biography.
   - If you spend more than an hour on screens each day (not for work), replace some of that time with reading a magazine, conversing with a neighbor, or listening carefully to a piece of music. Actually, do anything away from screens, and your capacity for attention will expand.
   - If you find it impossible to break out of your party bubble, go out of your way to hear a lecture by someone you know you'll disagree with. Take a friend who will probably like it. Grab coffee and conversation.
   - If you have convictions about any subject, subscribe to a podcast that will challenge your most treasured assumptions.
4. Take seriously "felt needs" around you.
   - Conduct a survey of your neighborhood (either in person, online, or both) that gets at the heart of your target audience's biggest felt needs, concerns, and longings. Publish the results to your group and to a public platform.
   - Ask your nearest local officials if there are any problems they simply don't know how to solve. Figure out something to do about it.

RECOMMENDED READING

Dalton Kehoe, *Effective Communication Skills,* DVD (Chantilly, VA: The Great Courses, 2011).

H. Richard Niebuhr, *Christ & Culture* (New York: Harper & Row, 1951).

Os Guinness, *Fool's Talk: Revovering the Art of Christian Persuasion* (Downers Grove: InterVarsity Press, 2015).

SLOW TO SPEAK

1. Read the "book" of Job as it was intended to be heard: As an epic poem.
    *   If you can't read it one sitting, take it in big chunks.
    *   Notice the "air time" each character is given.
    *   Pay careful attention to the disciplines of listening and speaking evident in the chief characters.

    For groups:
    *   Read as much as possible aloud by assigning parts to the chief characters plus a narrator.
    *   Visualize the content of Job using multicolored Post-it notes:
        -assign a color to each main character and the narrator;
        -write a chapter number on each note;
        -affix the notes in order upon the wall.
    *   Consider: *Why did the poet choose to structure his epic this way? Since Job is a wisdom book, what wisdom is being commended to us? What were the Jews meant to learn about their God from this story?*

2. Discuss Niebuhr's five categories of Christian approaches to culture.
    *   Summarize them using the pages referenced in the footnotes or by reading its Wikipedia article
    *   Do a bit of homework: What major theological schools or luminaries represent the various approaches?
    *   If you were to place yourself in one of the categories you feel most describes your current conviction, which one would it be? Why?
    *   Do you dispute Niebuhr's assessment? If so, what's he got wrong? What is missing?

3. Critique some "Jesus" films.
    *   What are a few films about the life of Christ that you have seen?
    *   How does the portrayal of His life compare with the written records in the New Testament Gospels?
    *   How might these films have been used as propaganda?
    *   Are any of these films "good films," despite their assumptions and message?

- What's the use of such films? That is, should Christians even make them?

In a group:

- Watch a film about Jesus and share your reactions (critique the film, not each other).
- Assign a different film to your various members to watch and report.
- Discuss the questions above.

4. Increase your courage. Pretend you're the next street preacher on the corner:
   - What would you say? Write it out. You never know when the chance will arrive!
   - How would you say it?
   - What would you objectives be?

5. Is there someone you love whom you've yet to tell about your faith in Jesus?
   - Write them an old-fashioned letter.
   - Take them out for a drink and ask them if you can share about your faith.

RECOMMENDED READING

Bryan Chapell, *Christ-Centered Preaching: Redeeming the Expository Sermon* (Grand Rapids: Baker Books, 1994).

Eugene Peterson, *Tell It Slant: A Conversation on the Language of Jesus in His Stories and Prayers* (Grand Rapids: Eerdmans, 2008).

Makoto Fujimura, *Culture Care: Reconnecting with Beauty for Our Common Life* (Downers Grove: InterVarsity Press, 2011).

William R. Baker, *Sticks & Stones: The Discipleship of Our Speech* (Downers Grove: InterVarsity Press, 1996).

IN THE FLESH

1. Compare and contrast the typical nuclear family in America with the extended family of Naomi found in the story of Ruth.
   - What advances, if any, has our modern world brought to bear on household life?
   - What wisdom can we glean from such an ancient Jewish model?
   - Is there anything about Boaz's approach to covenantal living that would be impossible, implausible, or undesirable today?
   - Is there anything about the scenario in Ruth that we desperately need today?

2. Describe in five minutes or less all three aspects of your current household situation (if you're single, describe your shared living situation or your most current experience in a household of any kind):
   - Its structure: Where do people fit? Who is who and why?
   - Its moral dimension: What behaviors, words, and attitudes are clearly unacceptable? What is celebrated and encouraged?
   - Its culture: What does it smell like, for real (physically)? What are its prominent moods? How would you describe the psychological atmosphere? What contributes to its particular culture?

3. Imagine the ideal household culture.
   - Describe its typical day.
   - List the contributions it would make to its immediate neighborhood.
   - Consider the costs involved.
   - Imagine how its existence would be threatened.

4. Very often churches cater to nuclear families.
   - What are the worthy motivations, conscious or not, of this "focus on the family?"
   - What unintended consequences have occurred because of this this focus?
   - In your experience, if your background in Christian, how has your earthly household intersected with God's household (the church)?

5. List the groups of people in your region who are most vulnerable as a result of broken family structures, lifestyles, or cultures.
   - Which groups are presently receiving an appropriate level of concern and help? Who's helping?
   - Which groups are being ignored? Why is this? What can be done?
6. A question in the form of a metaphor: Should Christians be putting their cultural muscle into preventative measures or into emergency first aid? That is, is it more important to create conditions for cultivating healthy households, or to pick up the broken pieces from dysfunctional families? Why?

RECOMMENDED READING

Robert Farrar Capon, *Bed and Board* (New York: Simon & Schuster, 1965).

Thomas Howard, *Hallowed Be This House: Finding Signs of Heaven in Your Home* (Medina, WA: Alta Vista College Press, 1976).

Edith Schaeffer, *L'Abri,* revised edition (Wheaton: Crossway Books, 1992).

Margie L. Haack, *The Exact Place* (Memphis: Kalos Press, 2012).

IN THE FAITH

1. Read Jesus' high priestly prayer found in John 17, and consider:
    - Are you inclusive of other faiths or exclusive toward them?
    - What are Jesus' main concerns, in this prayer, for His immediate disciples and those who would believe through their message (presumably us)?
    - What is it about America that seems to encourage such a diversity of denominations, splinter groups, and even home churches?
    - Would an honest assessment of your current region conclude that Christianity is unified, fractured, in crisis? Something else?
    - How are you pursuing love toward fellow Christians? That is, in what ways does it come *un*naturally, and you need God's help?
    - Describe a moment when you felt loved by a body of Christians.
    - Why are you hesitant to invite people to your local church?
2. Skim through the section showcasing examples of cultural engagement.
    - Do you find any of them satisfying or disturbing?
    - What kinds of intentional engagement do you respect in your region?
    - What kinds of engagement are utterly misguided, needing improvement, or completely missing?
    - If you were suddenly richer by ten million dollars, and you had a dozen full-time workers on your team, what kind of enterprise would you launch? Or, if you're not a start-up type, what kind of enterprise would you like to be a part of?
3. Let's talk about church *"meh"*mbership. It used to be that Americans were largely in favor of institutional alliances such as church membership. In recent decades there has been a verifiable move to "personal spirituality," church hopping, and loose associations of Christian fellowship. Some even advocate digital church life.
    - What are the reasons you (or your tribe) give for questioning church membership?
    - Of those reasons, which ones hold the most water logically, emotionally, biblically, and historically?
    - Which ones are less noble?

- Discuss the various ways you and your friends "sign on the line" to join a group of people?
- What, after all, is involved in church membership? What should be involved? That is, what are both the benefits and responsibilities?
- Is our our current culture ripe for a return to trust in church as an institution? Or are we heading for further skepticism? Why?

RECOMMENDED READING

Robert Louis Wilken, *The Spirit of Early Christian Thought: Seeking the Face of God* (New Haven: Yale University Press, 2003).

John F. Thornton and Susan B. Varenne, Editors, *John Calvin: Steward of God's Covenant: Selected Writings* (New York: Random House, 2006).

Dietrich Bonhoeffer, *Life Together* (New York: Harper & Row Publishers, 1954).

Francis A. Schaeffer, *The Church at the End of the Twentieth Century* in *The Complete Works of Francis A. Schaeffer,* vol. 4: *A Christian View of the Church* (Wheaton: Crossway Books, 1982).

EARTHLINGS ARE ENOUGH

1. Unpack the image of God as a concept. Read Genesis chapters 1 and 2 deliberately, hovering over the verses that speak directly about humanity (1:26-ff; 2:5-9; 2:15-ff). Compare and contrast the two accounts of the creation of humankind:
   - What do chapters 1 & 2 emphasize in their own ways?
   - What does humanity share with the rest of creation? What is unique about humanity?
   - What would you say is the fundamental ontology (the very essence) of being human?
   - How do you see the effects of "the fall" today?
   - How did you react to the section of this chapter where Jesus quotes Psalm 82, calling people "gods?"
   - What was He trying to say to His fellow Jews?
   - Do you think people today have too low or too high a view of humanity?
   - How well are Christians in your community utilizing the bridge of humanity to proclaim Christ?

2. How real is digital reality?
   - In what ways is social media a legitimate extension of our humanity?
   - How is it a reduction of our humanity?
   - Pretend you rule the world. What are some screen-time guidelines you would pass on to: parents of toddlers, junior high girls, college guys, newlyweds, parents of high schoolers, or empty-nesters.
   - What future digital platforms (such as Airbnb, Uber, and Facebook) do you foresee coming online in the next ten years? Will people adapt to the digital landscape in a healthy way?
   - What is the next ubiquitous boom after the digital revolution? Bio-tech? Artificial Intelligence? Cancer-free living? Clean fuels?
   - Can Christians be on the forefront of those emerging realities? If so, how?

3. Take a Bodily Inventory (It's not what you think). Find two sheets of paper, not the digital kind, the tree kind. Take up a writing instrument, and hold it squarely between your forefinger and thumb.

- Consider your yesterday: Write down what you did with your body during each half hour for a 24 hour period. Start and end with your bedtime.
- Consider today: Where will you body take you? What position will you be in? Describe your likely moments, physical needs, and posture toward you world in the most corporeal terms possible.
- Examine your sheets: If an alien were to fast-forward a video of your bodily experience, what would stand out to him? Do you see any patterns you didn't expect? Does this inventory concern you in any way? What does your bodily experience tell you about: What you like the most? What you love the most? Who you fear the most?
- If you are in a group, describe one of your days, showing your bodily inventory. Share any general observations. Defend yourself (!). Field questions from your group, if you dare.
- How are our bodies and our spiritual experience linked?
- What kind of bodily experience should a mature Christian long for, exhibit, and desire for others?

RECOMMENDED READING

James K.A. Smith, *You Are What You Love: The Spiritual Power of Habit* (Grand Rapids: Brazos Press, 2016).

C. John Collins, *Did Adam and Eve Really Exist?: Who They Were and Why You Should Care* (Wheaton: Crossway Books, 2011).

Barbara Brown Taylor, *An Altar in the World: A Geography of Faith* (New York: Harper Collins, 2009).

C.S. Lewis, *The Weight of Glory and Other Addresses* (New York: Simon & Schuster, 1962).

Marilynne Robinson, *Home: A Novel* (New York: Farrar, Straus and Giroux, 2008).

Frederic Drimmer, *Very Special People: The Struggles, Loves, and Triumphs of Human Oddities* (New York: Amjon Publishers, Inc., 1973).

NOTHING IS NOT SACRED

1. Going back to Paul and Barnabas' encounter with the Greek pagans, what about that story disturbs you? Heartens you? Confuses you?
2. If you were handed the mic at the Pride Fest, which is sort of what happened to Paul, how would you address the crowd? Could you and should you build a bridge to the biblical story?
3. Considering the tribe of people you find yourself in, and considering your own cultural context, ask yourself these questions:
   - Who are we, culturally speaking?
   - How have we been raised?
   - What do we value?
   - How do we spend our time and money?
   - What do we think other groups of people see in us or dislike about us?
   - Who do we care about (as evidenced by our actions, not necessarily our sentiments)?
   - Where are we?
   - What are the questions being raised publicly within our region and our population?
   - What can we do to get on the bridge with our neighbors to create a dialogue about what matters most around here?
   - Where might we make the greatest impact: Amidst immediate needs? In the coming year? Toward long-term solutions?
   - What interests and resources (people and otherwise) exist at our disposal?
4. Here is a helpful exercise I picked up from Q Ideas. The point is to train you to think realistically and restoratively about anything under the sun. It can also be a lot of fun and lead to some critical action points. Plug any popular idea, cultural expression, or human institution into this matrix of questions, and see where it takes you. In a church class I was teaching on social apologetics, I invited my audience into some improvisational cultural analysis. I asked them to toss up any human endeavor they could think of so that I could run them through these questions. One gentleman volleyed with "tagless underwear." That was meant to stump me, of course, but I like surprises and a good laugh, so I said I thought the phenomenon

was probably good for saving on production costs but possibly confusing
for those getting dressed in the dark.
- What is good about it? That is, how does it contribute to human
  flourishing?
- What is bad about it? That is, how is it actually harmful to people?
- What is confusing about it? That is, how does it need clarification?
- What's missing in it? That is, what can be done to improve it?

RECOMMENDED READING

Augustine, Bishop of Hippo, *The City of God* (New York: Random
  House, Inc., 1950).
Abraham Kuyper, *Lectures on Calvinism* (Grand Rapids: Eerdmans,
  1970). *Originally given as the Stone Lectures at Princeton University, 1898.*
Tolkien, J.R.R., *The Fellowship of the Ring* (New York: Houghton Mifflin
  Company, 1994).
Gabe Lyons, *The Next Christians: The Good News About the End of
  Christian America* (Colorado Springs: Multnomah Books, 2010).
Dick Keyes, *Seeing Through Cynicism: A Reconsideration of the Power of
  Suspicion* (Downers Grove: InterVarsity Press, 2006).

LOVE THE ONE YOU'RE WITH

1. What are cities and towns good for? We all know that most of the world has been urbanizing since the Industrial Revolution. In America, the population growth continues around our metropolitan areas. Talk about the good and the bad regarding dense population centers:
   - Where in America is the population growing? What are the sociological theories that explain this shift?
   - Where in America is the population declining? What are the sociological theories that explain this shift?
   - Do you agree that Tim Keller's three reasons explain why Christians appear to be moving back to cities?
   - Does Tom's fourth reason make sense to you? Does it go too far?
   - Should local churches try to bridge the cultural gap between town and country, city and suburb? Or should they lean into their setting?
   - Should church leaders address the topic of geography, or is that better left up to the individual's conscience? That is, should a "theology of place" have a place in the life of the church? If so, how?
2. Take stock of your own built environment:
   - What physical setting do you call home? Urban, rural, suburban?
   - To what degree is your lifestyle integrated or disintegrated, according to this chapter's use of those terms?
3. How does your setting affect your sense of happiness, contribution, or anxiety?
4. How does your built environment affect your ability to engage your culture?
5. Be the bridge.
   - What opportunities does your place easily afford for meeting people on the human bridge?
   - What bridges are missing?
   - Are there bridges to nowhere you must avoid or overcome?
   - What repairs are needed on the bridge to create better engagement?

6. Film in Place: Did you ever notice how many films center on a particular place? Just a cursory scrub through this author's mind reveals a few:

    Paterson: A bus driving-poet revels in the mundane beauty of his urbanized New Jersey streets.

    Blade Runner (original or *20149*): A bleak, rain-drenched metropolis sizzles in electronic despair.

    Avalon: An immigrant family disintegrates in parallel with its upward mobility out of Baltimore into the suburbs.

    The Lord of the Rings trilogy: An arduous, life-alternating quest returns Frodo and gang to Hobbiton.

    The Apartment: A laid-up photographer becomes a voyeur and hero overlooking a solitary courtyard.

    Manchester by the Sea: Entrenched New Englanders eek out a life on a rocky shoreline.

    Cars: Radiator Springs gets bypassed by an interstate highway, but as luck would have it . . ..

    The Tree of Life: Mysterious, llimitless divine providence touches on Waco, Texas. Mind blown.

    Most RomComs: Set in New York City, often in the Upper West Side.

    Can you think of any other films that explore a particular place on the map? (The titles are often a giveaway).

    • Compile a bucket list of films that center on a particular place.

    • Make a goal to watch one each month. Consider visiting the film's actual or storied location. For instance, if you want to visit Preston, Idaho, you will find the backdrop for *Napoleon Dynamite*. This author rides his bike past a row of porches in Lancaster City almost daily where a scene from *Girl Interrupted* was filmed. IMDB.come is an outstanding resource for scouting out locations depicted in films.

7. For a group: Gather to watch one of the above movies or another that reveals the impact of place upon its story and characters. If possible, match the film's ethos to your viewing situation. For instance, if it's an urban film, watch it at someone's house in the city, and take a walk afterwards. Follow suit iff it's a country or suburban setting. The Himalayas may be difficult, so use your common sense. Discussion suggestions:

• What is the main assumptions this film makes the importance of place?
• How do the characters feel about their place? How does it affect their longings, choices, and relationships?
• Is the film maker making a value judgment (albeit subtly) about a particular kind of place?

RECOMMENDED READING

Jane Jacobs, *The Death and Life of Great American Cities* (New York: Random House, 1961).

Craig G. Bartholomew, *Where Mortals Dwell: A Christian View of Place for Today* (Grand Rapids: Baker Books, 2011).

Garrison Keillor, editor, *Good Poems, American Places* (New York: Penguin Group, 2011). Selected and introduced by Keillor

Wesley Hill, *Spiritual Friendship: Finding Love in the Church as a Celibate Gay Christian* (Grand Rapids: Brazos Press, 2015).

Andres Duany, Elizabeth Plater-Zyrberk, Jeff Speck, *Suburban Nation: The Rise of Sprawl and the Decline of the American Dream* (New York: Farrar, Straus, and Giroux, 2000).

LIFE'S A PARTY

1. From what you know of the Old Testament writings, what was the purpose of the weekly Sabbath, the Jewish feasts, and the Year of Jubilee? That is, what was God's intention for the Israelites?
2. Moving on to the New Testament, read Jesus' view of the Sabbath from Matthew 12:1–8.
   • Again, what's the purpose of God's day of rest?
   • How had the leaders of Jesus' day, in His estimation, perverted the Sabbath?
3. If it's true that "the Sabbath was made for man" and not the other way around, how would that apply to the rest of the Ten Commandments? Go ahead, take them in turn, and consider what it means that humans weren't made for God's law; instead the Law was made for humankind's good.
   • E.g., Men and women weren't created to serve marital and sexual fidelity in some abstract way; instead, the law governing sexuality was made for their good.
   • E.g., People weren't created to make God feel better by worshiping Him; rather, the prohibition against idolatry was given to ensure God's children remained free of less worthy masters.
4. In your experience, is the Sabbath (Sunday, Lord's Day,) a fast or a feast?
5. Grab a copy of *The Screwtape Letters* by C.S. Lewis, and read chapter 11 aloud. (Keep in mind, this book is a fanciful take on temptation in letters from a senior devil to an apprentice; "The Enemy" referred to is the Christian God).
   • Screwtape describes four types of humor. Define each and give a current example.
   • Would you add any to our postmodern experience of comedy?
6. Regarding flippancy, the most "effective" type of humor for leading someone to hell, Lewis reveals the darker side of the human heart: "[Flippancy] is a thousand miles away from joy: it deadens, instead of sharpening, the intellect; and it excites no affection between those who practice it ..."
   • Do you agree with him?
   • Have you fallen prey to flippancy, cynicism, or joyless laughter?

7. What are some of your favorite comedy shows or films?
   • How would you categorize their type of humor?
   • Do any of them lead you to a deeper sense of joy as a child of God? Why?
   • Do some leave you wanting a shower? Why?
8. What is the funnest activity you've been to in the past month?
   • What were its key elements?
   • What was its purpose?
   • Did your laughter make you feel closer to God?
9. Who are some of the most celebratory people you know?
   • How do they do it?
   • What can you learn from them?
   • How can you "exploit" their spirit?

RECOMMENDED READING

Desiderius Erasmus, A.H.T. Levi, editor, Betty Radice, translator, *Praise of Folly* (London: Penguin Classics, 2004).

C.S. Lewis, *The Screwtape Letters* (New York: The Macmillan Company, 1953).

Bob Goff, *Love Does: Discover a Secretly Incredible Life in an Ordinary World* (Nashville: Thomas Nelson, 2012).

Garrison Keillor, *Lake Wobegon Days* (New York: Viking Press, 1985).

BECOME A CHILD AGAIN

1. Read Psalm 8 out loud. If you are in a group, use a call and response: The
   leader reads the first half of each verse, and the rest read the second half.
   Then discuss:
   • Imagine David's position at the moment of writing this song. What was
     he doing?
   • What is he celebrating about humanity?
   • What is he celebrating about God?
   • What's the significance of verse 2? "Out of the mouths of babes and
     infants, you have established strength because of your foes ..."
   • Should a gaze into the heavens make us feel small or grand? Why?

2. Read from the letter to the Hebrews in the New Testament, chapter 2,
   verses 5-9. You'll notice it's derived from Psalm 8. The writer is clearly
   arguing that Jesus is superior to angelic beings simply by His human
   incarnation.
   • How else is Jesus similar in experience to every other human being?
   • How was His experience of incarnation unique?
   • According to this author, what did He accomplish for us?
   • Take a moment right now and express your praise to Jesus in song.

3. Relive the past. You may have a lot of pain to push through. If that is the case,
   I'm very sorry about that. Still, there was a time and a place where you experi-
   enced childlike wonder, even in the darkest of circumstances. Consider your
   childhood before you learned to protect yourself from grown-ups. Put aside
   the triggers for painful memories, and find the triggers to joy.
   • Study some old photos. Look for smiles. Why are you smiling?
   • Visit your home town. Take in the smells of a simpler time.
   • Call an old friend, parent, or someone who has treasured you for a long
     time. Ask them to tell you the best stories.
   • Enjoy some kids. Borrow some if you don't have your own. If you are a
     young parent, know that you have my greatest sympathy, having raised five
     myself. In quiet moments, however, listen to them. What do you observe?
   • Get on the floor with some kids. Pretend, read books. Not because they
     need to be cared for but because you need to re-joice.

4. Enjoy the Divine Now.
    - Play hard with others. Join a sports league. Set out a board game or a puzzle. Do something useless for a change!
    - Prioritize your fitness and long walks. Rake a pile of leaves, and you'll know what to do.
    - Investigate an inkling—something you'd like to learn about or do one day.
    - Get a counselor. So much of the therapy we need is recovering the joys of childhood and healing the pains of the past.
    - Talk to someone. Share your concerns, fears, and dreams with a close friend. Emotional maturity only comes when we honestly deal with things.
    - Tell someone what they're worth to you and to God, especially if they struggle with a sense of guilt, shame, or unworthiness.
5. Prepare for the future.
    - Read great fiction. The longer the books the better. Try Tolkien or Tolstoy. Get lost. Immerse yourself in an utterly "useless" universe such as the Harry Potter series or Shakespeare.
    - Read some children's books. Read them to children. Read them to the retired.
    - Read the Bible, not as fiction, but as fictionalized nonfiction. Notice the authors' styles, let the stories affect you. Picture God as the Master Storyteller and the Protagonist.
    - Fuel your imagination with beauty, goodness, and truth as a ballast against the coming storms. Go to a museum, or sleep under the stars, or watch people cross the street.
    - Look yourself in the mirror, and tell yourself: "Your name is written in heaven. God, your Father, treasures you. His world is waiting for you to finally figure out you are delighted in. Now, get going." What, now?

RECOMMENDED READING

C.S. Lewis, *Surprised by Joy: The Shape of My Early Life* (London: Geoffrey Bles, 1955).

David Brooks, *The Social Animal: The Hidden Sources of Love, Character, and Achievement* (New York: Random House, 2011).

A.A. Milne, *The Complete Tales of Winnie-the-Pooh* (New York: Dutton Children's Books, 1994).

Susan Schaeffer Macaulay, *For the Children's Sake: Foundations of Education for Home and School* (Wheaton: Crossway Books, 1984).

ACKNOWLEDGMENTS

I'd like to acknowledge my grown children first and foremost. Before they even knew how arduous their life was, and especially afterwards when they began to wonder if road trips in a sketchy VW Vanagon were a normal thing, my beloved five have been my favorite fans. Fandom includes constant reminders of my raspy voice, but it mostly involves a sweet and enduring lovingkindness I simply do not deserve. Katie, Eliza, Hannah, William, and Magdalena are my best friends (along with my new sons, Ben and Adam). I hope this book makes sense of their eclectic upbringing and emboldens them to continue living what Frederick Buechner describes as "the tragedy, comedy, and fairy tale" that is the Gospel.

I wouldn't be here without Dartt and C. Jeanne Becker, my beloved parents. They cultivated humor and a profound sense of individual expression and responsibility that equipped me with confidence to live life to its fullest. My in-laws, W. Frank and Wendy Johnson, were quick to enfold me into their Christ-centered home in the faraway land of South Jersey. What began as a shock to them ("You're dating that guy?") has become an untold source of encouragement to me through many years of vocational dysphoria. Parentally, I couldn't be more blessed. "To him who is given much . . .."

My mentors have tended to be writers and practitioners I've admired from afar. Many are quoted here. In terms of real, live heroes, I'd like to principally note C. David Green. He was my first trainer and boss in campus ministry, but his intentional fatherhood impressed me most. Dave embodies the axiom that animates me every day: "Be respected most by those who know you best." Dave has that respect. And for the record, his personality couldn't be more different from mine, and yet I dare say no one understands how I tick more than him. And, somehow, he likes me. Before Dave was Joe O'Day, my own campus worker, who told me if I didn't marry Becky I'd be crazy. Thanks, Joe. I went to Covenant Seminary to learn from Jerram Barrs, my living connection to L'Abri and Francis A. Schaeffer. I admired him mostly from afar and ended up being greatly influenced by his protégé, Wade Bradshaw. Wade's Schaeffer lectures in local bookstores put the bee in my bonnet about public exposure of the Christian worldview. Sheepishly (I'm sure), he even allowed me to give a lecture on the Elephant Man. Another fellow with a different Myers-Briggs pattern from me is C. John "Jack" Collins. One of the toughest professors (and not a little scary to first-year Hebrew students), Jack won my coveted Favorite Professor award. I've kept his massive, cogent, and pastoral syllabi from each class, and still refer to them. Our pastor in St. Louis, George Robertson, exemplifies for me the love necessary for each communicative event. Between him and his mentor in preaching, Bryan Chapell, I learned what preaching could be, and I've been chasing after love in Christian proclamation ever since.

Joy Strawbridge was once a promising writing student of mine when she was in ninth grade. For this book, she served as my initial editor, but her greatest contribution was uncovering my best voice: "I think the way you want to say that is …." Also, to Byron Borger, I must give credit as chief whistle-blower on a few passages that were out of step with my intent. Ever since I threatened to write a book ten years ago, his excitement, insight, and friendship have been priceless. Please visit Hearts & Minds Bookstore often.

I want to thank the many generous supporters of The Row House: faithful attendees of our concerts, forums, and other various events—as well as past and present board members. Standouts include: Ned Bustard—his partnership has been energetic, selfless, and utterly indispensable; Rob Ilderton, who led the charge for my recovery from ministry burnout by believing in me; Chris and Carol Clark for hosting me so I could free-write for a week—I recaptured a bit of my childhood while playing with their kids and digging Yacht Rock with Chris; Mark Crutcher and Kimberly Ibarra for putting the screws to me about writing this book (and helping to make it possible, too); and Matthew Monticchio for listening to me with an ear trained to the soul, teaching me the language of music, and making me laugh so hard it's embarrassing—if that were possible. I don't have room to thank all my Forum speakers by name. They number nearly one hundred men and women. Their faces have graced our posters, and their presence formed the nucleus of our forums. Thank you for letting me show you off, and for helping me build a platform for "engaging current culture with ancient faith."

About the time our kids were flapping out of the nest, along came Rue. My days would be drudgery without her nutsy smile, lust for fetching, and dogged devotion. Lastly, I want to acknowledge the secret of my boyancy: Pennsylvania autumns, the Susquehanna River, and teaberry ice cream.

Tom would like to thank the following friends who participated
in a pre-order campaign to jump-start this book:

Bryan & Lydia Baird

Joe & Judy Braymer

Henry Bleattler

Jessica Bodene

Joanne Brown

Ian & Julia Busko

Jeremy Chen

Mark and
Rebecca Crutcher

Tim and Jenny Everett

Daniel Gagliano

Adam & Bridgette Grim

Rick Hennessey

AJ & Aftan Hoffer

Tim Hoiland

Joseph & Tenli Hunter

Kimberly Ibarra

Bruce & Lorie LaSala

Hannah Eagleson Matias

Matthew and
Becky Monticchio

Katherine Nellis

Richard & Lisa Nyguist

Matt Seilback

Daniel Seymour

David & Sue Smith

Daniel & Claire Southwell

Brad Steele

Hannah Vogel

. . .

And just for fun, some of the friends chose to add a dedication:

Good Posture? That was the
least of our worries with Tom.
Have you heard of M-80s?
—C. Jeanne Becker

What she said. And have you
checked the oil in that thing lately?
—Dartt M. Becker

Like a mobius strip: both sides
at once, and a twist that gives life
a simple but mysterious unity.
—Rev. Benjamin T. Inman, Ph.D.

These courses, like a page of
prancing poetry, fair gallop with
the rocking-rolling rhythms of their
maker's mind. Twill a jolly pleasure
be, twixt song and soaring harmony,
its canters so to quaff.
—Jonathan Gray, Esq.

Thanks for asking SCORE Lancaster-
Lebanon be part of this journey.
—Eric Parker, The Row House, Inc.
business coach

Tom and Becky Becker have been
great encouragers of Friends of L'Abri
Nashville, and we are excited about
our friend and advisor's first book!
—Rob Wheeler, MDiv, MAC

Tom has written a must-read book
for anyone interested in engaging
current culture with ancient faith.
Read this book and learn what
creativity, civility, hospitality, and
warmth can look like.
—Duane Otto, Founding President,
Ithaka Fellowship

THE ROW HOUSE

Now that you've read my first-ever book, please discuss it with your friends. And if you're in town, swing by one of The Row House Forums. Or if you're too far away, drop me a line. I'd love to visit you in your context, talk on the phone, or do something fun like speak at a retreat—perhaps even host a forum for you! I'm easy to find at tom@therowhouse.org, or sitting on the front porch in the West End of Lancaster, juggling civility, hospitality, humanity, and creativity . . . all the while trying to practice good posture.

THEROWHOUSE.ORG

SQUARE HALO BOOKS

... EQUIPPING THE SAINTS FOR
CULTURAL ENGAGEMENT

The Beginning: A Second Look at the First Sin
"[An] engaging discussion on the nature and consequences of the
original sin using the biblical accounts as his primary authority....
A sound background in scripture, a solid presentation of his positions,
and generous application make this book a very good reference on
the subject." —*The American Journal of Biblical Theology*

Bigger on the Inside: Christianity and Doctor Who
Like the TARDIS itself, the fantastically popular series *Doctor Who*
is bigger on the inside, full of profound ideas about time and history,
the nature of humanity, and the mysteries of faith.

Intruding Upon the Timeless: Meditations on Art, Faith, and Mystery
"A collection of brief essays by the editor of *Image,* a distinguished
journal of religion and the arts. A nice mix of the whimsical, provocative, and devout, as befits the variegated subject."—*First Things*

Revealed: A Storybook Bible for Grown-Ups
"*Revealed* sets out to crush any notion that the Bible is a safe,
inspirational read. Instead the artwork here, historic and contemporary,
takes a warts-and-all approach to even the most troubling passages,
trading well-meaning elision for unvarnished truth."—J. Mark
Bertrand, novelist, speaker, and founder of the Bible Design Blog

Serious Dreams: Bold Ideas for the Rest of Your Life
Edited by Byron Borger, this collection of insightful commencement
speeches is full of ideas that will help you live out your calling in
God's story and pursue serious dreams.

Teaching Beauty: A Vision for Music & Art in Christian Education
"*Teaching Beauty* is a must-read for school administrators, teachers,
education majors, and all who seek to encourage the next generation to engage in creativity and beauty." —Dr. Robert F. Bigley,
Executive Director of The Trust Performing Arts Center

LEARN MORE AT
SQUAREHALOBOOKS.COM